C000183748

Finding a Job

How to Plan Your Career

Sarah Berry

WARD LOCK

A WARD LOCK BOOK

First published in the UK 1997
by Ward Lock
Wellington House
125 Strand
LONDON
WC2R 0BB

A Cassell Imprint

Distributed in the United States
by Sterling Publishing Co., Inc.
387 Park Avenue South, New York, NY 10016-8810

A British Library Cataloguing in Publication Data block for this book may be obtained from the British Library

ISBN 0 7063 7610 2

Designed and typeset by Ben Cracknell Studios.

Printed and bound in Great Britian by CPD (Wales), Ebbw Vale

Contents

ONE

Introduction to Career Planning

A career is not what you find but what you *create*. Many people view those who have a fulfilling career as 'lucky': in fact, what they are really saying is that a particular person is luckier than they are. But what the onlooker fails to recognize is that these so-called 'fortunate people' have made it that way – they have created opportunities and situations for themselves in order to maximize their potential and achieve self-fulfilment, and they have made their own luck. For the onlooker, it seems easy: but is it?

Successful people claim time and again that they are just ordinary people, who simply did what was natural and important to them. In short, they had a vision and took steps to achieve it. It is therefore in your interests to develop a vision and a plan that will dig you out of the rut, give your career meaning and propel you forward. If it hasn't happened to date, now is the time to be positive, because your future looks bright. Equip yourself for great things and you will achieve them – but it won't happen overnight.

What is a career?

There is more to a career than having a job. A job is something you do every day, but a career is far more long term and means having a purpose, perhaps of achieving personal advancement or success in life. So, having a job doesn't necessarily mean you have a career: in a career there is a common thread between each job, and each job is one step towards achieving your ultimate goal. And because a career is far more long term than a job, it must involve planning.

Career planning

Career planning is like looking into a telescope, seeing something a long way away and bringing it forward. Thus, in simple terms, career planning is the ability to look into the future, to visualize where you want to be and what you want to have achieved, and then to plan the necessary steps to your goal. However, before you can take these steps you need to be fully aware of your strengths, weaknesses, skills, expertise, potential and desire for success.

These days, career planning is not just for the career minded: it is an essential requirement if you want to fulfil your potential, achieve long-term satisfaction and avoid derailment. (Derailment is the process whereby business careers are terminated because they are no longer valued by their organization. The career may be ended through redundancy or purely because an individual is no longer considered for promotion; Chapter 2 will demonstrate how to avoid derailment.) Today's job market is uncertain. No job is secure, jobs are constantly being cut and contracts are often rewritten. There is no such thing as a job for life, so to win through in this market it is necessary to be a realistic career strategist.

This book will take you through the process of career planning step by step, showing you how to create a career vision and determine the route needed to achieve it. The benefit to you will be that planning your career will enrich your life.

TOP TEN REASONS

WHY PEOPLE DON'T PLAN THEIR CAREERS

Most people find it difficult to plan their career properly, so they simply avoid doing so. They are thus avoiding doing what is actually best for their career. Bearing in mind that a career can span as many as 40 years or more, it is pointless to work at something you don't enjoy for that length of time, so a career without a plan can be regarded as a car without any wheels: it won't get you very far and could cause you a lot of frustration in the meantime!

More often than not, it is not that people don't want to plan, but that there are certain 'barriers' that get in the way and prevent the individual from improving his/her performance or career possibilities. In reality, however, these barriers don't exist, because they are mental rather than physical limitations which individuals place upon themselves because they lack self-confidence or self-belief. Normally, these barriers have been built up over a number of years and so they are perceived as huge obstacles, but once a person realizes that they can change their way of thinking, these 'barriers' become as vulnerable as their thoughts. Thus, if someone thinks something might be possible, it is far more likely that they will give it a try and consequently succeed, because they know that it is possible to do so.

Read the list below and check whether any of the barriers to career planning apply to you. If they do, you will now be aware of what is preventing you from taking that first step.

1 Self-belief.

Many people fail to succeed in their career because they lack belief in themselves, their abilities and their potential. If you don't believe in yourself, how can you plan for greater things? On the other side of the coin, there are others who do believe in themselves and seem to get where they want to be. The truth is that, on the whole, most people could achieve far more if only they believed it were possible.

The reason why most people don't achieve more is that they fail to recognize their own individual potential. They find it easier to see the potential in others, and tend also to live and perform within the boundaries placed upon them by their spouse, partner, family, tutors and bosses. Thus, in order to fulfil your potential you need first to believe in yourself; in addition, people generally like boundaries, as they feel comfortable within their own self-imposed constraints – but the successful see boundaries as barriers to be overcome rather than limits to hold them in.

It is not vain to believe in yourself, and if you do, so too will others. A contact of mine once told me how a throwaway comment from the person who recruited him spurred him on throughout his career: 'I see within you a tremendous desire to succeed. Don't throw that away, and one day you will be sitting in my chair at the top of this organization, managing and directing all these people and projects', the person predicted, and 30 years later he had fulfilled the prediction. So, if someone has predicted great things about you, don't be in too much of a hurry to reject them.

If you do not have the advantage of drawing upon predictions or inner confidence, then you will need gradually to build up your self-belief. Try to change your attitude to situations that you would normally dread or avoid: instead of saying what is in the left-hand (negative) column below, try saying what is in the right-hand (positive) column.

Negative	**Positive**
I can't.	I can.
Nothing ever goes my way.	Life is good to me.
I haven't the time to do that.	I'll find time to do it.
You don't understand me.	I haven't expressed myself clearly.
I'm not changing my mind.	I think we have different views.
I'm not trying that again, last time it all went wrong.	I want to make it work this time.
I have a lot of experience.	I can learn something new every day.
I didn't do very well at that.	With a bit of practice, I can improve my performance.
I don't think anyone is listening to me.	I think we can be reasonable and work something out.

Remember, if there is something you are worried about give it a try, because it may not be as difficult as you have made it out to be – and if you don't try you will never know whether or not you can do it.

Some employers recognize the need to boost their employees' confidence from time to time by sending them on training or retraining courses, so try not to dismiss out of hand something that could be in your best interests. Graduates are often put through an initial intensive 'training' course where they are expected to carry out very different and sometimes quite daunting tasks – for example, rock climbing, white river rafting or abseiling – and the comment afterwards from participants is often 'I would never have thought I could do that!' Courses are often a great opportunity to boost an individual's self-belief, as within a group environment people will attempt what they once thought was impossible, at least for them.

Learning something new can be exhilarating, especially in a group situation. However, in work people are often asked to do something new without the support of a tutor or group. On these occasions, a person may attempt the new task but make the fundamental mistake of not supporting their best interests: they are often too hard on themselves, judging their first attempt at the task against other people who have far more experience and knowledge than they do. Be careful not to judge your worst points against someone else's best points; for example, if it is your first time chairing a meeting, then congratulate yourself first rather than immediately criticizing your performance, reflecting on how things went only the next day, when the emotion has had time to subside. Note the good points about the meeting, and *only when that has been done* note also the points that need improving. In this way you allow yourself to grow through experiences, rather than shrink.

In summary, practise believing that you can, and you will maximize your skills and potential.

2 Lack of knowledge.

Knowledge is the key to career fulfilment: if you know what is required to succeed within your career, it is far easier to plan and therefore achieve it. Initially, securing a job is about having the right kind of qualifications and a suitable personality. However, whether or not you succeed within your career and get chances to move along the career track is dependent on much more subtle characteristics. These include:

- ✔ Performing within your roles.
- ✔ 'Fitting in' with the company culture and its requirements.
- ✔ Gaining recognition for what you do.
- ✔ Being regarded as an expert at what you do.
- ✔ Being seen as having more to give and not as someone who has reached their potential.
- ✔ Being regarded as a reliable, trustworthy and credible employee.
- ✔ Having a reputation to be proud of, as it is this that will lead the way.

However, people often forget that a career is about continuous building rather than isolated jobs and instances. It is about increasing your knowledge and building up a portfolio of skills and experiences, which are the kinds of assets that companies need and value. So often, people forget the building bit and get carried away by their emotions and what seems a good idea at the time. For example, people start their career on a certain track and are quite happy for a while. Then they might think it is time to move on, or they may be pushed involuntarily by the company, or they may think they should be doing something better or earning more. This is often when mistakes are made: people dive into jobs without assessing the impact this could have on their career, and they do this because they haven't the knowledge and therefore the ability to make that all-important career decision. Chapter 5 of this book will show you how to gain that knowledge and Chapter 6 how to assess the next career step.

Career advice is difficult to obtain and consequently most people find out the hard way, by making the wrong kinds of choices and having to live with those decisions. What makes career planning so difficult is that it is hard to generalize about careers; after all, everyone is an individual and has their own aims, aspirations and goals. Chapter 3 provides a Career Questionnaire which will help you to establish your career aims and focus on the areas that need to be worked on before you make the next move.

As knowledge about career advancements is hard to come by, people often look for outside input to help them plan their career. However, as you can see from the list below, this can have serious drawbacks if you don't approach it in the right way.

- **Your company** can offer a valuable service in planning your career. Most people, however, fail to benefit from their company in this way because:

✗ **They don't take charge**. Some employees make the mistake of believing that their company is responsible for organizing, planning and sorting out their career. Companies lose interest in employees of this kind: the onus is on the individual to manage his/her own career, as the company doesn't have the time to think about and consider each person's individual needs and problems. Regardless of your skills, experience and technical knowledge, you run the risk of alienating your employers if you can't or won't take responsibility for your own career development.

✗ **They become too self-orientated**. Companies tire easily of employees that talk purely in terms of their own needs, for example demanding a higher-grade job, more perks, or claiming they deserve this or that. Organizations want employees who are committed to the business, not those who are committed to lining their own pockets. Talk in terms of your benefit and value to the business and you will probably gain what you want anyway.

✗ **They are a threat to the business**. Employees can become a threat to any business if they are:

  - *Not committed to their job.*
  - *Unreliable.*

- *Inflexible.*
- *Emotionally unstable.*
- *Irrational.*

Or if they:

- *Make unreasonable demands, perhaps about their future.*
- *Upset the balance of the team.*
- *Have an inflated sense of their own importance.*

In short, employees can become a threat if their behaviour, attitude or relationships with others affects their performance. If you are a threat to the business, your own position could be threatened.

The company's primary concern is to run a profitable business which offers a valuable, effective and professional service to its customers. As long as you can appreciate the purpose and demands of the business as a whole, take responsibility for your development, and ensure that you are a valuable asset to the company, the rewards will be there for you. Focus on building up an impressive portfolio of skills and performing within your current job: remember, a company will only invest in you if you are prepared to invest in them.

- **Employment agencies** are in the business of placing people in jobs which they have been asked to fill by their client companies. These agencies offer a valuable service, but be aware that if you ask for *career advice* they could offer it on the basis of the jobs they currently hold on their files.

- **Outplacement services** are generally brought into businesses at certain times, usually when the company is making large-scale redundancies. Many of my clients have had experience of outplacement companies and felt that they regarded employees as numbers on a file rather than as individuals, but this is dependent upon the company and the particular circumstances.

- **Spouses, partners and family** are often called upon to offer career advice from time to time. Be aware that people close to you are emotionally involved and also may have no real perception of how you behave or conduct yourself at work. Consequently, their advice can be useless or the opposite of what is actually required.
- **Career advisory centres** tend to talk in terms of professions and their requirements rather than the individual, their career to date and exploring the next steps.
- **Books** on career planning are scarce. Often the subject forms part of another topic, so it is glossed over at great speed. There are a lot of books written on the subject of 'Getting to the Top' or 'Once at the Top'; however, the vast majority of people simply want to know how to maximize their potential and achieve a fulfilling career, and if the top is in sight then they can choose whether or not to go any further! This book focuses on planning the best career possible for yourself, so relax and enjoy the prospect of learning a new skill – one which you can put into practice as soon as you have completed the book.

3 Role model.

Having a role model is an easy and worthwhile way in which to develop a career. Most people, however, don't have one because they fail to recognize the significance of having a person whom they can watch closely to see how he/she deals with different people, situations and problems. In this way, you can improve your own performance by drawing upon your role model's successes, failures and short cuts. The benefits of having such a person far out weigh the effort that might be required to build a close relationship with them.

Who can be a role model? The answer is that anyone can be your personal role model: a relative, friend, personal contact, a current boss or a previous one. More important than who this person is, is what this person does for you and your career, so the emphasis is on learning and progression and not on being 'pals'. In order for someone to be your positive role model, certain criteria apply. You need to:

- ✔ Respect this person's technical competence.
- ✔ Be able to talk openly with them without feeling that you are being patronized, taken advantage of or manipulated.
- ✔ Be able to gain experience and knowledge from them.
- ✔ Respect their leadership style.
- ✔ Be aware of their reputation.
- ✔ Be sure that this is the right person from which to learn.

The reason for these stringent criteria is that you are effectively trying to emulate and learn from your role model, and if this person is *not* respected within their profession do you really want to be like them at all? This is especially true if you are modelling yourself on your current boss, as you don't want to be too closely associated with someone who isn't going anywhere within the organization, or you probably won't be going very far either!

Your boss is the most obvious person to have as a role model, but it doesn't always work out that way. Sometimes a boss may be a difficult character or not willing to develop other people's careers. In order to overcome this hurdle, try to establish why he/she is being so difficult. Is your boss nervous that you are waiting in the wings to replace him/her? Does he/she take you for granted? Is he/she particularly manipulative? Whatever you decide is the reason, try to realize that there are advantages in this type of experience, and you can learn how to win through by being persistent and determined. These types of hardships are part of success training, so learn to stand up to your manipulative boss by saying 'no' – repeatedly if necessary – especially if he/she is taking you for granted. Use your judgement, and normally in a company that values its employees you will pull through.

If your boss doesn't set an example you want to follow, then look for an alternative role model. It is worth bearing in mind that most people are flattered by having a protegé who respects and wants to learn from them. The role model will then pass on tips and offer advice, and in doing so will give the protegé valuable knowledge that could help him/her save time, energy and effort in the long run. However, be aware that at some point most role-model relationships run out of steam. There comes a time when the relationship ceases to be as effective as it once was: perhaps the protegé has become over-dependent on the role model and has lost sight of his/her own ideas, beliefs and style, or maybe the role model has no more to give to the protegé. Perhaps the role model has reached the limit of his/her usefulness, or it may be that he/she needs to pursue different tasks. Therefore, always review the effectiveness of your relationships, and where possible replace one role model with another in order to maintain momentum and personal growth.

4 Dedication/desire.

Many people lack the dedication required to plan their career. From time to time they may become fired with enthusiasm and make certain changes, but before long, events, personal circumstances or outside activities start to distract them and the focus swings away from their career on to something else. An ex-headmaster summed this up by saying, 'It is always the pupils that didn't perform in their examinations that turn up years later with the biggest grins and the flashiest cars. Strange, isn't it, but they all tell me how they had to prove themselves in the world of work.' Success in the world of work is based upon wanting to succeed and putting in the necessary effort.

There is no secret formula to success. It is a matter of fixing your mind to it, being committed to your vision and plan, and working at it – for example, most olympic athletes put their success down to doing nothing but sleeping, eating and living their sport. However, apart from being dedicated you must also set yourself realistic targets. Targets which are either too high or too low will cause you unnecessary disappointment or dissatisfaction. Think in terms of the steps required to achieve your 'dream' job, then take one step at a time – and remember that all great achievements have a simple beginning.

The difference between success and failure is small, but that difference is in an individual's desire, commitment and dedication to *winning*.

5 Open mind.

Planning and managing your career requires a degree of flexibility, as it won't always run according to plan. This sounds like a contradiction, but it is true. This is often the point at which people stop planning because they feel that it doesn't work; however, this has more to do with their attitude to what has happened to them than with the event itself. The section on Attitude in Chapter 2 (see pages 24–32) gives advice on how to triumph over defeat, despair or disappointment.

There will always be obstacles along your career routes or reasons to give up, but whether or not you can handle these depends on how open minded you can be. Avoid telling yourself that something is impossible and try to view situations differently. Focus on the 'whole picture' and on how all the pieces fit together: doing this will help you to differentiate the 'wood from the trees' and start to see things you had previously never noticed. It will also help you to focus on yourself as part of the whole organization rather than just an individual, and this is vital in terms of career progression.

A contact of mine told me how someone within their organization was laid off because he couldn't cope with the changes the organization had implemented: 'It was sad, Roger was dismissed because he just failed to change with the times. He still wanted to do what the company had always done, but he failed to recognize the benefits these changes had brought.' You must avoid restricting your career possibilities because you are fearful of change. Times of change are also times of opportunity, so how you manage your career will depend on how open minded you can be.

THIS BOOK WILL DEMONSTRATE

1. **How to recognize your potential.**
   Direct your career in accordance with your skills and expertise.
2. **How to manage and control your own career.**
   Don't rely upon unreliable sources such as luck, other people or emotion.
3. **How to dig yourself out of a rut and realign your career.**
4. **How to think about and visualize your long-term career.**
5. **How to find and secure an unadvertised job.**
6. **How to build inspiration and assess the next career step.**
7. **How to determine whether a change of career is a possibility.**
8. **How to avoid the pitfalls of a new job.**
9. **How to increase your value.**
   And consequently your market rate (salary).
10. **How to establish yourself as an expert within your chosen field.**
11. **How to establish just how career minded and motivated you really are.**
12. **How to make your dream become a reality.**
    What may have appeared impossible before is now possible!

In order to plan effectively you need to have self-belief, knowledge, a role model, dedication and an open mind. The only cost in obtaining these assets is a bit of effort on your part, while the benefits will be enormous in giving you a boost and the energy to plan a brighter future.

TWO

Why Plan?

Plan your career and you will remain in charge of it. Planning helps to avoid some of the career pitfalls such as failing to keep up to date, to adjust to changing business requirements or to remain a valuable part of the organization. Planning has a very positive effect as it enables you to monitor your progress and realize your achievements, and it keeps you motivated during difficult spells.

These days, organizations encourage individuals to take charge of and plan their own career. Company structures are flatter than they were 20 years ago as technology, computerization and experience have all contributed to making organizations slimmer: it is not unheard of for there to be only three or four tiers between the very junior and senior members of management. Thus, career progression doesn't always mean a step up. Far more importantly, it involves the building of long-term relationships and the calculated collecting of key skills and expertise, which may entail moves sideways or even backwards in order to move forwards. The key is always to concentrate on gaining the necessary skills. These skills may be technical, managerial or personal.

Remember also that it is impossible to stand still within an organization. The business world is like a moving floor, and in order to survive businesses have to move with the times and grow. So, if you do commit yourself to staying in the same job, remember that you have to move forwards in order to stand still. This chapter covers the types of planning you could adopt, and the career pitfalls to avoid.

The importance of planning

Planning is vital because it:

- ✔ Ensures that your career is driven by your plan and not your emotions. It prevents your being tempted to hop from job to job, to make rash decisions and to apply for almost anything that comes up.
- ✔ Minimizes the risk of making mistakes – mistakes cost time and could cause unnecessary hardship, so they are worth avoiding. Any career gap, illogical move or change in direction will have to be explained at appraisals or interviews.
- ✔ Provides you with long- and short-term goals, and keeping these in mind helps to maintain your focus and thus ensure completion. Clarifying your goals can help to keep expectations about a particular job realistic.
- ✔ Makes it easier to stay on course, and to measure and celebrate success. It is a good idea to have a written record of career aims and aspirations; reference to these during a low patch can boost your morale and also help you to recognize just how much you have achieved to date.

If you plan rather than simply hope for good things to come your way, you will direct your own career and thus create your own luck. Many of my clients have referred to career opportunities as 'being in the right place at the right time'. This myth, however, puts the ownership on something else rather than on the individual, and it is true that luck often has its part to play in the course of our lives, but you have to be able to recognize and grasp an opportunity when it arises. Some people have plenty of 'luck' dangling in front of them but they just don't read it that way: they might see it as a problem, whereas someone else might see it as an opportunity. Remember, it is how you interpret a situation that is important. In addition, opportunities are more likely to occur if you are, so to speak, in more than one place at a time, so make yourself visible outside your immediate work circle and recognize the importance of 'networking' (see pages 81–84). Concentrate on making your own luck and weighting the dice in your favour, and things may happen sooner than you expect.

Planning ahead

How far ahead should you plan? This is the burning question, and unfortunately there is no set answer. It has more to do with what you feel comfortable with, but remember that the more time and effort you invest in your career, the greater the rewards. As far as the options open to you are concerned, you may prefer to have:

- An overall career strategy. This will highlight possible job areas you want to work in and where you hope to finish your career. People who have a highly focused and clear vision of their career tend to be those who have completed an intensive work-related course of study – perhaps a degree or a professional qualification – in their subject; they have the advantage of knowing already which aspects of the work they prefer and where their expertise lies. There are also those who have a close relation, colleague or friend already in the profession to whom they can share ideas and discuss careers to date, and they will be able to design a career strategy earlier on than someone without this personal contact.
- A plan for a specific time period, say five years. Often people choose this option when they are unaccustomed to planning, when they are restarting their career after a break, when they change career direction or if they are in an industry which is undergoing radical change. Under these circumstances, it would be shortsighted to plan a future which could be irrelevant five years down the line. A short-term plan of this sort helps to keep the individual focused during the period of change, but also allows flexibility and time for reconsideration. With such a plan, it is always best to start planning the next stage at least a year before the original plan expires.

- A plan which looks only as far ahead as you can look back. This type of plan is particularly relevant for the new starter. For example, if you have just finished a three-year study course, or perhaps your GCSEs, it is advisable only to plan a few years ahead, because after two or three years in a full-time job people are usually much clearer about what they want and aspire to be doing. Newcomers to the job market are keen to get on and excel at what they do, but try to avoid being too rigid about what you want because experiences will change you, and what you want at 18 or 21 may not be the same at 24 or 28. Newcomers are also particularly 'green' about business possibilities and timescales, so a lot has to be learned within a short space of time. Ease up on what you think you *should* be doing and establish a feel for what you *want* to be doing. Remember: only time will tell.

Above all, whatever type of plan you choose, it should not be a static document. Review, revise and change your plan in line with your ideas, desires and aims. To be effective, a plan should change as you mature. Remember also that in certain professions the environment is a moving field. To take a poignant example, many jobs now in existence within Aids nursing would not have been around ten years ago, and let us hope that the need for them will one day disappear. There is no real certainty as to where some of the jobs of the future will lie, but as long as you change with the times you will come through.

Career pitfalls

A career pitfall sounds more serious than it really is. It is actually a period of time when you might feel that your job/career is not all it is cracked up to be and you might therefore make a disastrous career move at this point. Firstly, it is important to be aware that your career can very easily change, and circumstances, events and situations can occur that alter your attitude towards it. Secondly, bear in mind that there is no such thing as the perfect job, but some jobs have more favourable aspects to them than others.

A contact of mine once told me how he was always being told by others that he was so fortunate to have such a super job. 'Without doubt, I enjoy my work. I thrive on my job and it constantly gives me a buzz,' he told me, 'but I always tell people that on balance 90 per cent of my job is the run-of-the-mill stuff and only 10 per cent of the work is all that exciting. But it is that 10 per cent that keeps me gripped to the job.' For this person, the 10 per cent was enough to keep him out of the rut. However, you should remember that any job can become a bore if you let it – something you do every day rather than something you enjoy. If this is the case, you are probably not enjoying your life to the full and are bogged down in all the details. You may even lack energy, motivation and the ability to express your individuality. Minor irritations can grow out of all proportion and everything becomes a big effort – even getting up in the morning. Recognizing that you are stuck in a rut is crucial, for you can do something about it – and straight away.

If you are in a rut you most certainly *do not* want to move into the wrong job. When people are in a rut they don't think rationally or view situations clearly, and they will often take action that can be detrimental to their career just because they want to escape from their current situation. The key is to be careful. The following sections describe the career pitfalls and how to avoid them.

Pitfall 1: Attitude

Being in a rut can reflect in your attitude, and attitude is fundamental to career progression. If you have the right kind of attitude, the opportunities will be there for you. Get your attitude wrong, and you can *do* no right!

The wrong attitude means that career opportunities diminish, and could eventually result in your being pushed aside. Many people underestimate the significance of attitude in building their career; they dismiss it as basic, and perhaps even wrongly assume that they have the right kind of attitude. However, attitude is the basis upon which good management and careers are built, so be aware that if you dismiss its importance a company could then dismiss you or your career.

Attitude Traps

Working long, hard hours is not enough to ensure career progression: you also need to be aware of and sensitive to the needs of others, to mix and to get on with everyone. The reason for this is that doing the work is only one part of the equation: your value is based upon your output and your contribution to the company, and your behaviour and attitude will have an effect on others, thus either increasing or decreasing their output. There is therefore no escaping the fact that you are part of a group and that you affect the team as a whole. Remember also that as you become more senior within an organization, you will be assessed more on the team you manage than on your own performance. There therefore needs to be a balance between personal productivity and relationships with others in order for you to reach your full potential – so attitude can either make or break your career!

Building and maintaining good working relationships with everyone, in good or bad environments, is what is required, but some people fail to do this. Sometimes emotion and feelings run high and affect people's relationships with others; some people are just too self-orientated and think only of themselves; others are so ambitious that in their quest to get to the top they trample on those in their way; while others are simply naive and have no real idea that their attitude is visible to others. Listed below are the attitude traps that it is easy to fall into, and which will affect who you are and how you contribute to the organization.

✗ **Blaming others** for what is not happening or coming your way is one of the easiest traps to fall into. Often people feel that they are due a promotion, a company car, an increase in salary or personal recognition, and when this doesn't arrive hurt feelings, damaged pride and wounded self-esteem can all send the individual into a downward spiral. Energy is put into reconfirming and building upon the 'hurt' rather than into working out how to achieve what they want. When people blame others they tend to share their feelings, and this in turn affects the attitude of the people around them, so that fellow employees also begin to lose their enthusiasm and motivation, with the result that a blame culture then develops.

✗ **A childish attitude** can turn the employee into a liability to the company rather than an asset. People with this attitude have the idea that the company owes them a living, safety and a future, so that the company is given the role that their parents once had and has to look after them and ensure their well-being. The individual becomes so cushioned by the company that he/she soon becomes incapable of making his/her own decisions. This type of attitude can weigh down the company and be a burden to fellow workers, who may have to do some of the person's decision-making for them.

✗ **A threatening attitude** is often adopted by the person who is used to getting his/her own way. He/she may even have used this approach in the past and succeeded. A threatening style is where the employee places his/her demands on the table with certain conditions attached, normally along the lines of 'Give me this or that, or I'll leave'. This is a very risky approach, for companies soon tire of demanding employees – who often regard themselves as something better than they really are and use their aggressive approach to try to get what they want. The attitude tips on pages 28–32 demonstrate that other approaches are just as effective.

✗ **There are losers** and winners in life. Winners enjoy winning, but they also accept that losing some of the time is par for the course: losing doesn't finish them off. Instead, they dust themselves off, pick themselves up and try again. Losers, on the other hand, lose most of the time and unfortunately attract even more losers around them, so one 'bad apple' can cloud the atmosphere and cause productivity to drop. Losers are people who give up easily, are quickly discouraged and think negatively. For example, a loser is someone who presents a new idea and when it is rejected crawls into his/her shell, loses momentum and finds it hard even to perform the job. This new state of mind is then transmitted either verbally or non-verbally to those around him/her by the person's withdrawn state, making it difficult for co-workers to remain positive. The 'bond' between them thus becomes one of *protection* rather than *production*. Losers are therefore valued far less by organizations than are winners, as they are regarded as parasites on the productivity of others.

✗ **A destructive attitude** usually occurs when the individual feels angry/hurt/frustrated by circumstances but also trapped within that situation, helpless to do anything or take alternative action. He/she then literally turns against the company and sets about getting back at the organization. Normally the person will show his/her disapproval of the company by being awkward for the sake of it, refusing to do certain things or perhaps even taking it one step further and disclosing confidential information or policies. However, this attitude rarely works, because the company will usually have more power than one lone individual, and the individual is making himself/herself even more powerless by becoming ineffective.

✗ **An 'historical' attitude** is one whereby a person's past affects their present state of mind and therefore the future. In fact, it is a fear of change or a refusal to develop and grow with the times. For example, some people hang on to their past failures and draw upon these in times of change or doubt: they often say that they weren't very bright at school, so haven't got this and that and therefore can't do such and such. However, what happened in the past doesn't have to happen in the future: what is past is past, and as yet the future lies untouched. Refer to the section on self-belief on pages 9–11 and try to avoid letting your past rule your future – especially when you may not have liked what happened in the past anyway!

Do you have an attitude problem?

Above we listed the key attitude problems, one or more of which you may or may not recognize in yourself. To some extent, we all have attitude quirks, because none of us is perfect. However, problems only arise when the quirk becomes so predominant that it affects the way we deal with, treat and mix with others. Unless something has been pointed out to us it is often difficult to see our own faults, and even when something is drawn to our attention it can be hard to face up to, as we all like to think of ourselves as almost perfect. Therefore, the easiest way to work out whether or not you may have an attitude problem is through the following exercise.

Think of yourself in the work situation. How do people react to you and treat you? Has anything ever been pointed out as a problem with your attitude, maybe a comment at an appraisal, a remark at a meeting, or maybe you have overheard something? People may have referred, for example, to your failure to listen, to report mistakes or to self-motivate (see page 32). Write it down, whatever it is: this is not the time for reflection on whether it is true or false.

If you find it difficult to remember things that have been said, think about people you know within the organization. Who is there that drives you mad? What particularly is it about them that you find difficult to take? Write it down, including all their attitude faults and failings. People often find it easier to recognize in others faults that they actually have themselves, so before you scrap your comments, think again: could it be that the faults you see in the person you find so difficult to work are actually your own as well?

Improving your attitude

Listed below are three key ways to improve your attitude by being positive and building working relationships. Following these steps is one easy way to keep your career afloat; most people don't adopt them and consequently their career stalls, so get one step ahead of the competition by putting into practice what you read below.

Developing a positive approach

A positive attitude is a real asset. Some people can instinctively push unpleasant thoughts out of their mind, while others dwell on the negative. The key is to try to focus more and more on the good rather than the bad.

Attitude is something which other people notice and management comment upon, so build up a positive attitude by practising the following techniques:

- ✔ **Practise being positive** and try to focus on one aspect of your job at a time. By starting to make positive thoughts a habit it will be only a matter of time before you begin to reap rewards from your new attitude.
- ✔ **Talk about positive things at work**. A negative attitude winds up some people and is not appreciated by others. Your colleagues will regard you as a negative person if you moan constantly about the bad aspects of your job.
- ✔ **Search for the 'good' in others**. Everyone has positive features and attributes, so look for these, and spread the good word about others. Think nice thoughts about people and it is far more likely that this will be reflected in others.
- ✔ **Focus on what you like about your job and company**: is it the people, place, location, environment, culture, policies, or product? Begin to be proud of what you do and who you work for.
- ✔ **Don't let others distract you**. Try to avoid letting other people's negative thoughts affect you. Accept that you can only change yourself; if other people want to be negative, let them. At least then there is room for people to see the difference between you. Above all, preserve your own positive attitude.

Building good relationships

Having a positive attitude can help you to create positive relationships with your boss, your colleagues and others within the organization. Relationships exist at work because you have chosen to work for your company; the thing to remember is that at work you cannot chose who you mix or bother with, so the key is to get on with everyone! Relationships can be either strong or weak ones, depending on the effort and time you invest in them and also on how you react towards other people – if you don't bother with certain people, either ignoring or avoiding them, this will hamper your relationship with them. Remember also that just as you perceive people in certain lights, others too are making similar judgements about you based upon their own upbringing, experiences, insecurities and likes and dislikes. Relationships can therefore be difficult to manage, control and influence.

Your relationship with your boss

Your relationship with your boss is crucial to your career development, and the most beneficial relationship to have is a good and open one where there is an unrestricted flow of thoughts, ideas and observations. If you or your boss begins to withhold information, then the relationship cannot develop and will eventually break down. Of course, he/she may not be your 'ideal' boss or provide the leadership you prefer, but he/she will certainly influence your career. Whatever kind of boss you have, ideal or not, the onus is on you to:

- Build the relationship between the two of you.
- Be perceptive and understanding of the pressures on your boss.
- Give the relationship time and the benefit of the doubt.
- Work efficiently and effectively under his/her direction and leadership.

Never underestimate the importance of your boss in developing your career. A contact of mine once told me how he had been prepared to allow one of his key managers to move from the central to the provincial head office on account of a change in his personal circumstances: 'I agreed to the proposal because this person had taken charge of the situation and suggested a possible solution to his problem, rather than coming to me and moaning about it'. The key is to keep your boss in the picture and never underestimate his/her power to influence your future.

Relationships with colleagues and others within the organization

These relationships need to be preserved and kept healthy as well. The way to do this is to avoid concentrating solely on your relationship with your boss, or on building relationships with only one or two colleagues and neglecting the rest, so you should devote equal time and energy to all your daily relationships. In addition, you also need to create and sustain relationships outside your own department.

In developing and building relationships with other workers, concentrate on being one of the team. To be a valuable team member, try to conform to all decisions once they have been made; try to work well with everyone; and openly contribute ideas to ensure the success of projects on which you are all working. Avoid criticizing the team leader, because some of the blame will always come back on you. After all, you are a member of that team – aren't you?

Repairing relationships

Relationships are vulnerable things and can be damaged by people being careless, insensitive or distant. Most relationships have to be worked on continually to keep them alive and productive.

However, when a relationship breaks down each party will have their own belief as to why this occurred and they often blame the other party. To restore the relationship, one person has to give way, approach the other person and break the ice. The best course of action is for you to forget about who was in the wrong and set about restoring the relationship; otherwise, your career could be damaged by your colleague or boss seeking to gain the upper hand. Bear in mind also that time spent on a broken relationship could be spent on far more profitable things, so, repair the relationship as quickly as possible by:

- Viewing career success as having good working relationships. Remember also that you never know when you might need this person's support, so bury the hatchet.
- Identifying the cause of the conflict: for example, was one of you under a lot of pressure? If a cause can be found, it is a lot easier to forgive and forget.
- Having an idea of how you will rebuild. Can you accept some of the blame? If you can, then swallow your pride and take action, especially if the relationship is important to you. Alternatively, perhaps you could take the heat out of the situation by injecting a bit of humour into the discussion, but avoid ridiculing the other person.

Give it a try and you may end up gaining a lot of respect for making the effort to sort out the situation.

Dealing with criticism

Everyone has faults and is reminded of them from time to time. The key is to admit to your faults and put them right, otherwise they could damage relationships further. First, consider whether the criticism is of a one-off mistake on your part or a persistent fault. If the latter, take time to sort it out. Some tips are given below for solving the three most common failings.

Failure to listen. If you find it difficult to concentrate or merely to wait for the person to finish before you start talking, then you are probably not a good listener. Become an effective listener by:

- Looking at the person talking to you.
- Jotting things down if you are liable to forget.
- Asking questions if you don't understand.
- Reflecting back on what has been said to ensure you heard correctly.

Failure to report mistakes. Everyone makes mistakes from time to time, so you will be in good company. A mistake won't damage your career, but it could cause you unnecessary embarrassment if you try to cover it up. Don't be afraid to admit your mistakes, because others will respect you for doing so.

Failure to self-motivate. Motivation is the willingness to do whatever is required in order to complete the task. Initially it may take a bit of effort, but if you apply yourself it can be done. This book will also help you to think long rather than short term, so that you can ride the 'plateau' periods (when things slow up) in a career.

Pitfall 2: Golden Hellos

A 'golden hello' is the second most common career pitfall. This is the process of choosing a job for its grade, perks or status rather than assessing its potential. To assess the appropriateness of a job, you need to understand how the job fits into the organizational structure; how important a role it is; what the next step is from this job; what competition there would be; and how you compare with this competition in terms of skills, expertise and technical competence. In short, before taking a job, assess whether it is the right career move for *you*. Unbelievable as it may seem, this is an easy thing to overlook, especially if you have let your attitude slip a bit and are keen to escape from your current job.

However, you will all too quickly become accustomed to a higher salary, better car or increased recognition, and the attractions of the job itself also become the norm, to the point where it loses its original appeal. Self-fulfilment is based on being active rather than passive in what you do each day, what you can change or influence in a job, what achievements you can attain, and what targets and goals you have for the future, so a career driven by gifts, perks and money can lead to isolation and disillusionment. After all, once you've got it, where do you go next? Golden hellos can therefore limit rather than expand career possibilities, and the reasons for this are explained below.

- **Cul-de-sacs**. Choosing a job for its perks rather than its potential can draw you into a career cul-de-sac. Often there is no way out of this situation other than to retrace your steps, and even take a step backwards in terms of the package, or to step into another cul-de-sac and risk making the same mistake again. It is not uncommon for people to make career moves based solely upon the package, but they often fail to anticipate the stress involved or the toll that this can take on their personal circumstances.

- **Further irrational moves**. A golden hello is normally an irrational move, but it sets the trend for further irrational moves in the future, and once a habit has started it is harder to break. Rash career moves can damage a profile which has taken years to build. Remember: it takes far longer to build a reputation than to destroy one. Irrational career moves demonstrate to a prospective employer a dislike for what the person is currently doing rather than a desire to do the job on offer, so it is likely that employers will be cautious if they get a hunch that this is an irrational career move. Be aware also that what may appear to be a fantastic job has its downside as well – employers will obviously highlight the positive aspects of the job, because it isn't in their interests to focus on the pitfalls of the position on offer. Try, therefore, to look at both the good and the bad aspects of the job and then irrational career moves can be avoided.

- **Biting off more than you can chew**. A golden hello can persuade people to accept a job that they are incapable of doing, perhaps because they don't have the skills, background or experience required. Sometimes people even go so far as to change profession in order to receive bigger perks, and then find that they are constantly playing catch-up. This type of 'fingers crossed' career planning does not work in the long term, and the remaining chapters of this book will demonstrate how it can be avoided.

Pitfall 3: Business Awareness

Careers often run aground because people lack business awareness. They fail to recognize how they can benefit and add value to the business, and so after a while they don't. Too often, people think purely in terms of their job and their little empire, rather than of the whole process, input, output and profit. Frequently it is only when they are forced to take action, perhaps when they are laid off, that they actually do. So why don't people become business aware?

For many, it is pure laziness. For others, it is easier to pass the buck. Some people feel they can't, others are frightened to do so, and yet others don't know how to. However, everyone can learn something new, even if it is slowly. Bear in mind too that organizations tend to hang on to and have more time for those people who are committed and willing to put themselves out for the benefit of the company.

Confront what is preventing you from increasing your business awareness and the calmer you will be. Recognize that information is easy to obtain from the library or from company briefs in the form of leaflets, magazines, training, job descriptions, notice boards, bosses, colleagues and peers. Also try to read a weekly newspaper and trade journals. Open your eyes and ears, and absorb what you see and hear. Take an interest in the business and the company is far more likely to be interested in *you*.

Avoiding Career Pitfalls

You can avoid the major career pitfalls by:

- **Thinking strategically**. You are important, but in the context of the 'whole' organization, so avoid becoming 'self'- rather than company-orientated. This doesn't mean that you don't matter, because you do, but try to focus on what you want and then sell it in terms of what the company is pursuing.
- **Moving with the times**. Make the changes with the company, and where possible try to influence and be ready with those changes. One of the easiest ways to do this is to avoid remaining static in a job. Instead, build up new skills and expertise so that you are increasing your value, skills and reputation. It is comfortable to stick to what you are good at, but in the long term this is too shortsighted. Take the initiative and start to drive your own career forward.

Pros and cons of career planning

This chapter has shown how career planning is a necessity. It helps you to keep up to date, open minded and moving forward, and the advantages far out weigh the disadvantages.

DISADVANTAGES

Career planning can:

✗ Be a restrainer if you achieve what you want to in a shorter space of time than planned. It can be difficult to get the momentum going again, so you need a vision beyond the initial vision.

- ✗ Require a bit of effort.
- ✗ Be a de-motivator if you set targets too high and don't achieve them.
- ✗ Be difficult.
- ✗ Be quite tough on your patience.
- ✗ Be a bit of a chore.

ADVANTAGES

Career planning can:

- ✔ Help to focus the mind.
- ✔ Reduce drifting.
- ✔ Prevent irrational moves.
- ✔ Prevent unrealistic dreaming.
- ✔ Help to keep the focus on you, not others.
- ✔ Help to ride out the plateau periods.
- ✔ Help you to keep things in perspective.
- ✔ Keep you on your toes.
- ✔ Reduce the risk of derailment.
- ✔ Increase the likelihood of success.
- ✔ Help you to visualize your next move.
- ✔ Ensure that you move forward, not backward.
- ✔ Keep you up to date.
- ✔ Help you to assess *all* the information/facts.
- ✔ Help you to keep ahead of the competition.
- ✔ Keep motivation high.

Career planning is worth a try – now it is up to you to try it!

THREE

The Career Questionnaire

If you don't know what job you are looking for, you are not going to find it! The Career Questionnaire provided below is designed to help you think in depth about your career, establish how career minded you are and visualize your long-term career goals. By doing this, it will be far easier for you to pitch, design and develop a plan in accordance with your dreams, desires and potential.

The purpose of the questionnaire is to help you think beyond the superficial, obvious and simple issues, and to focus on your 'whole career'. It will help you to:

- Get to know yourself and your inner feelings.
- Understand the key career issues.
- Realize what you need to do more of or less of.
- Learn how to be effective and read your potential within your career.

The Questionnaire is divided into ten sections, under each of which there are between 10 and 30 questions for you to answer, with a total of 150 questions in all. Each question requires only a 'yes' or 'no' answer. However, once you have completed the questionnaire you will not get an overall score, as it is impossible to 'grade' a questionnaire of this kind. For example, it would be misleading to say that a score of 100 'yes' answers out of 150 is a good or an average score; what it is far more important to know is which questions you have answered with a 'no' and/or in which sections you have a particularly low total score, for it is these areas that need attention. This is therefore a personal and individual questionnaire which triggers you to think deeply and widely, to view your career as a whole, and to be aware of and consider things you may previously have dismissed. Once you have completed the questionnaire, add up the total number of 'no' answers under each section. Following the format given on page 54, write down all the things that need to be worked on, put right or developed in order for you to reach your maximum potential.

With a career, the onus is on you to direct and develop it as you wish. The summary at the end of each section is there to highlight and remind you of the key career issues that you may have lost sight of, but which need to be addressed if you want a fulfilling career.

So, have a go at filling out the questionnaire – you may be pleasantly surprised at the result, as your answers will indicate what you are doing right, as well as what you need to do in order to realign or improve your career. If you receive a 'nasty' shock and discover that the majority of your answers are 'no', do not despair. Try to establish where the problem lies: is it that certain sections have a very low score, or is it a more fundamental problem such as the need for you to change profession? If the former, work on one section at a time in order to avoid becoming discouraged. If the problem is to do with your profession itself, then pages 55–60 in Chapter 4 will offer advice in this area and the remaining chapters will explain how to make some of the transitions hinted at in the questionnaire.

The career questionnaire

This questionnaire will provide you with the knowledge that you require in order to plan your future. Read through each section and make an honest appraisal of your career to date. Although it may be time comsuming, it is a worthwhile exercise to explore every area of your career. So waste no more time and get to work on it!

1 Profession

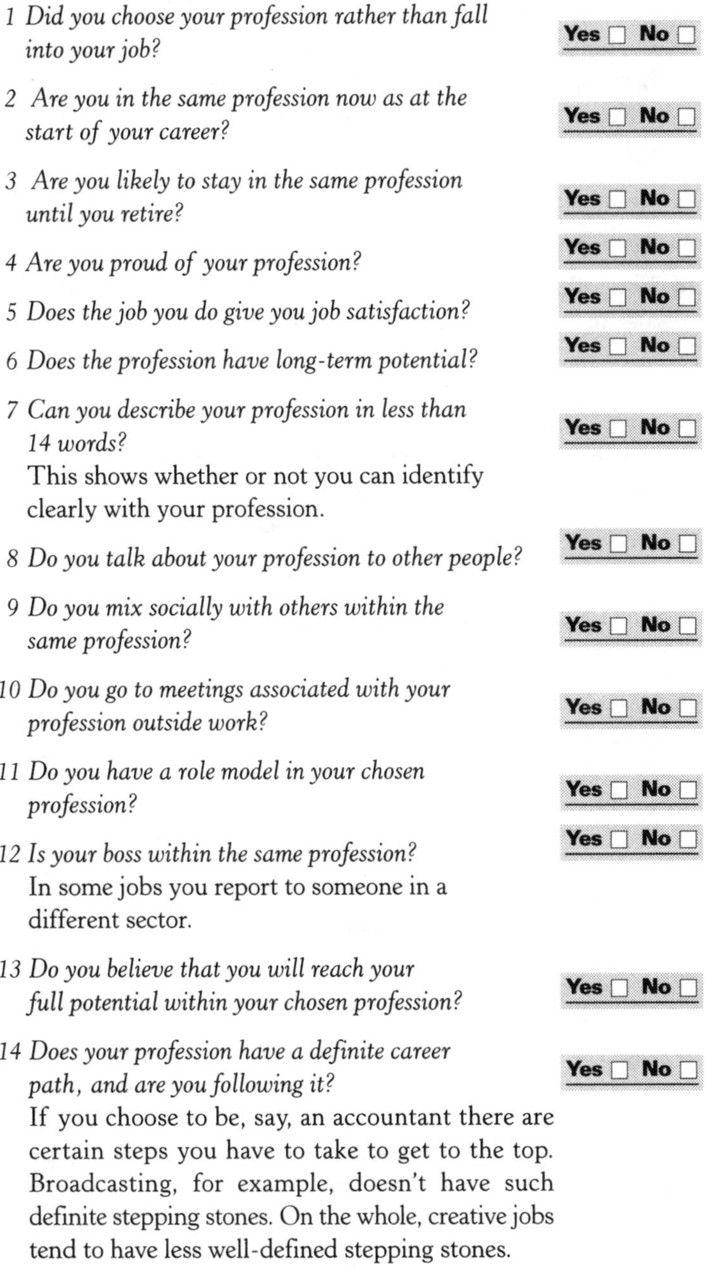

1 *Did you choose your profession rather than fall into your job?* **Yes** ☐ **No** ☐

2 *Are you in the same profession now as at the start of your career?* **Yes** ☐ **No** ☐

3 *Are you likely to stay in the same profession until you retire?* **Yes** ☐ **No** ☐

4 *Are you proud of your profession?* **Yes** ☐ **No** ☐

5 *Does the job you do give you job satisfaction?* **Yes** ☐ **No** ☐

6 *Does the profession have long-term potential?* **Yes** ☐ **No** ☐

7 *Can you describe your profession in less than 14 words?* **Yes** ☐ **No** ☐
This shows whether or not you can identify clearly with your profession.

8 *Do you talk about your profession to other people?* **Yes** ☐ **No** ☐

9 *Do you mix socially with others within the same profession?* **Yes** ☐ **No** ☐

10 *Do you go to meetings associated with your profession outside work?* **Yes** ☐ **No** ☐

11 *Do you have a role model in your chosen profession?* **Yes** ☐ **No** ☐

12 *Is your boss within the same profession?* **Yes** ☐ **No** ☐
In some jobs you report to someone in a different sector.

13 *Do you believe that you will reach your full potential within your chosen profession?* **Yes** ☐ **No** ☐

14 *Does your profession have a definite career path, and are you following it?* **Yes** ☐ **No** ☐
If you choose to be, say, an accountant there are certain steps you have to take to get to the top. Broadcasting, for example, doesn't have such definite stepping stones. On the whole, creative jobs tend to have less well-defined stepping stones.

Summary

- For career success you need a profession. A job is what you do, but a profession is your sector of work (for example banking, teaching, sales). Being a member of a profession makes it easier to progress, as it rules out the temptation to try a bit of this and that.
- Become part of your profession by living it, researching it and being committed to it.
- Find others within the profession to model yourself on and also to coach you when necessary.

2 Career to date

1 *Has your career to date been fast track – in other words, are you where you expected to be?* **Yes** ☐ **No** ☐

2 *Have you had a recent career appraisal?* **Yes** ☐ **No** ☐

3 *Are you more optimistic in your career now than when you started?* **Yes** ☐ **No** ☐

4 *Are you known 'externally' within your career among the press, other companies, and contacts?* **Yes** ☐ **No** ☐

5 *Are you known 'internally' within your career, so that people in the company, especially those in other functions, know your name?* **Yes** ☐ **No** ☐

6 *Is your career to date better than those of your contemporaries?* **Yes** ☐ **No** ☐

7 *Are you proud of your CV?* **Yes** ☐ **No** ☐

8 *Do you believe you have more potential?* **Yes** ☐ **No** ☐

9 *Are you satisfied with your career to date?* **Yes** ☐ **No** ☐

10 *Is there a common thread in your career to date and do your job moves follow a sensible pattern?* **Yes** ☐ **No** ☐

11 *Have people supported you in your career to date?* These could include spouse, partner, family, boss, colleagues and subordinates. **Yes** ☐ **No** ☐

12 Have you had any highlights in your career? **Yes** ☐ **No** ☐

13 Have you taken advice on your next career steps? **Yes** ☐ **No** ☐

14 Do you have a career mentor, someone with whom to discuss your career progression and opportunities? **Yes** ☐ **No** ☐

15 Are you in charge of your career (see question 16 for clarification)? **Yes** ☐ **No** ☐

16 Are you making your career decisions or is someone else doing this for you? **Yes** ☐ **No** ☐

17 Are you in the best job you have ever had? **Yes** ☐ **No** ☐

Summary

- Establish what you like about your career to date, including the companies you have worked for, your profile and training acquired. Focus on what you want to maintain in the long term.
- Be honest about your career dislikes, such as lack of recognition, support or personal growth. In order to move forward you may need to change certain aspects, and you need to be clear about what these are.

3 Career planning

1 Do you know what your next career move is? **Yes** ☐ **No** ☐

2 Do you have a definite plan for the next five years? **Yes** ☐ **No** ☐

3 Do you envisage being in a different job in five years' time? **Yes** ☐ **No** ☐

4 Do you envisage being with the same company in five years' time? **Yes** ☐ **No** ☐

5 Is your job secure for the next 12 months? **Yes** ☐ **No** ☐

6 Would it be difficult to replace you? **Yes** ☐ **No** ☐

7 *Do you scan through the papers regularly to see what your next career move could be?* **Yes** ☐ **No** ☐

8 *Do you have access to or receive copies of trade and professional journals at least one a month?* **Yes** ☐ **No** ☐

9 *Do you regularly read articles in your professional journal?* **Yes** ☐ **No** ☐

10 *Are you aware of how you could further your career?* **Yes** ☐ **No** ☐

11 *Do you need extra qualifications or skills for your next move?* **Yes** ☐ **No** ☐

12 *Is your profession secure (ie it won't undergo a major change) for the next ten years?* **Yes** ☐ **No** ☐

13 *Would you accept or have you considered a sideways move in order to gain broader technical experience and expertise?* **Yes** ☐ **No** ☐

14 *Would you relocate in order to develop your career further?* **Yes** ☐ **No** ☐

15 *Would you consider a foreign move in order to enhance your career?* **Yes** ☐ **No** ☐

16 *Do you need to gain new skills (such as an MBA, a foreign language, or computer experience) in order to enhance your career?* **Yes** ☐ **No** ☐

17 *Do you consider yourself to be the replacement for your boss?* **Yes** ☐ **No** ☐
If no, find out what you need to acquire in order to become this replacement.

Summary

- You need to plan for your future, not for the next moment.
- Establish whether or not you are unaccustomed to planning, resistant to change or an 'unstable planner'. An unstable planner is someone who changes all the time, being driven to plan when emotions run high or low, when he/she feels they should be getting further because everyone else is, or

when he/she finds it difficult to be in a lull. Chapter 7 will help to establish what motivates you, as well as what holds you back.

- Find our what qualifications and experience employers would require for your next job.
- Consider all the possible career options – retraining, foreign travel, a sideways move, acquiring new skills, an internal or external move. Above all, remember not to rule out something before you have assessed the option adequately.

4 Appearance

1 *Are you conscious of your company's business dress code?* **Yes** ☐ **No** ☐

2 *Can you differentiate between senior management and junior management by what they wear?* **Yes** ☐ **No** ☐

For men

1 *Do you buy a suit regularly, rather than waiting until the old one needs replacing?* **Yes** ☐ **No** ☐

2 *Do you wear a smart, up-to-date overcoat/ mackintosh?* **Yes** ☐ **No** ☐

3 *Do you wear a clean shirt every day?* **Yes** ☐ **No** ☐

4 *Do you polish your shoes at least twice a week?* **Yes** ☐ **No** ☐

5 *Do you only wear dark-coloured socks?* **Yes** ☐ **No** ☐
Brightly coloured or childish socks don't reflect well on you.

6 *Do you own more than two pairs of work shoes?* **Yes** ☐ **No** ☐

7 *Do you always keep your top shirt button done up?* **Yes** ☐ **No** ☐

8 *Do you ensure that your tie always covers your top button?* **Yes** ☐ **No** ☐

9 *Do you ensure that you don't suffer from underarm perspiration?* **Yes** ☐ **No** ☐

10 *Do you ensure that there are never any marks on or holes in your shirt collar?* **Yes** ☐ **No** ☐

11 *Do you always wash your hair regularly and avoid leaving it that extra day?* **Yes** ☐ **No** ☐

12 *Do you avoid using a disposable pen at work?* **Yes** ☐ **No** ☐

13 *Is your briefcase less than ten years old?* **Yes** ☐ **No** ☐

14 *Do you ensure you have a good shave each day, and if need be a second shave before evening meetings or social occasions?* **Yes** ☐ **No** ☐

15 *Do you have your hair cut regularly and avoid growing it too long?* **Yes** ☐ **No** ☐

16 *Do you avoid using paper handkerchiefs at work?* **Yes** ☐ **No** ☐

17 *Do you wear a number of different ties during the week?* **Yes** ☐ **No** ☐

18 *Do you make sure your tie never hangs short of your trousers by more than a couple of centimetres (one inch)?* **Yes** ☐ **No** ☐

19 *Do you make sure that you always file your work and never have a drawer in which you dump things?* **Yes** ☐ **No** ☐

20 *Is your desk always left tidy at the end of the day?* **Yes** ☐ **No** ☐

21 *Could you locate a file or other item within five minutes?* **Yes** ☐ **No** ☐

22 *Do you sift through your files regularly, scrapping unwanted paperwork?* **Yes** ☐ **No** ☐

For women

1 *Do you wear smart clothes every day?* **Yes** ☐ **No** ☐

2 *Do you have a separate work wardrobe?* **Yes** ☐ **No** ☐

3 *Do you have a spare pair of stockings/tights at work?* **Yes** ☐ **No** ☐

4 *Do you ensure that a damaged hem is mended immediately?* **Yes** ☐ **No** ☐

5 *Do you avoid wearing bright or vivid clothes to work?* **Yes** ☐ **No** ☐

6 *Do you always have clean shoes?* **Yes** ☐ **No** ☐

7 *Do you ensure that you never reveal the top of a stocking or let the top of a thigh show?* **Yes** ☐ **No** ☐

8 *Do you avoid wearing clothes that in certain lights reveal your underwear?* **Yes** ☐ **No** ☐

9 *Do you refrain from wearing heavy make-up to work?* **Yes** ☐ **No** ☐

10 *Are your clothes always clean and pressed?* **Yes** ☐ **No** ☐

11 *Do you have a suitable work briefcase?* **Yes** ☐ **No** ☐

12 *Do you avoid wearing fashion jewellery for work?* **Yes** ☐ **No** ☐

13 *Do you ensure that your white clothes remain white?* **Yes** ☐ **No** ☐

14 *Do you ensure that you spend less than ten minutes per day discussing your personal life?* **Yes** ☐ **No** ☐

15 *Do you ensure that your desk is left clean and tidy at the end of the day?* **Yes** ☐ **No** ☐

16 *Can you find something which has been asked for quickly?* **Yes** ☐ **No** ☐

17 *Do you avoid getting involved in excessive girlie chit-chat?* **Yes** ☐ **No** ☐

18 *Do you avoid crying at work?* **Yes** ☐ **No** ☐

19 *Can you hold your own with men and remain calm?* **Yes** ☐ **No** ☐

20 *Do you avoid getting pulled into a sub-meeting during or after a meeting?* **Yes** ☐ **No** ☐

21 *Are you unbiased about who you sit next to (ie you don't always sit next to your best friend)?* **Yes** ☐ **No** ☐

22 *Do you avoid the coffee rota syndrome?* **Yes** ☐ **No** ☐

Summary

- Spend time on yourself and others will invest in you.
- Dress in accordance with your company dress code.
- Be aware that clothes often reflect attitude and state of mind, so, if your clothes appear tired and worn out assumptions will be made about the wearer.
- Dress for success.
- Always behave in a professional manner at work and avoid being either too 'macho' or too 'girlie'.

5 Money

1 *Do you want to be in the top earning bracket?* **Yes** ☐ **No** ☐

2 *Do you have other work priorities than money?* **Yes** ☐ **No** ☐

3 *Over the last five years, has your income improved your standard of living?* **Yes** ☐ **No** ☐

4 *Do you avoid revealing details about your personal situation at work?* **Yes** ☐ **No** ☐

5 *Do you avoid disclosing your salary to family and friends?* **Yes** ☐ **No** ☐

6 *Can you envisage doubling your salary within the next five years?* **Yes** ☐ **No** ☐

7 *Are you happy with your previous salary increases?* **Yes** ☐ **No** ☐

8 *Have you ensured that your career options are not restricted by your financial situation (ie your money concerns are not a higher priority than your career)?* **Yes** ☐ **No** ☐

9 *Would you ever take a decrease in salary in the short term to further your career in the long term?* **Yes** ☐ **No** ☐

Summary

- Money is important, but just how important is only you can decide.

- Remember to keep your money matters to yourself, or you may invite unnecessary criticism, jealousy or antagonism.
- Money matters should be a lower priority than career issues.

6 Training

1 *Have you studied for a career-related qualification since leaving school/college/university and starting work?* **Yes** ☐ **No** ☐

2 *Have you signed up for and completed any adult education course in the last three years?* **Yes** ☐ **No** ☐
This demonstrates a desire to learn a new skill and acknowledges the importance of training and learning.

3 *Do you believe training would help you further your career?* **Yes** ☐ **No** ☐

4 *Could your career be advanced further by studying for an additional qualification?* **Yes** ☐ **No** ☐

5 *Do you have the time to study for an additional qualification?* **Yes** ☐ **No** ☐

6 *Has your boss/company recommended that you study for an additional qualification?* **Yes** ☐ **No** ☐

7 *Was training discussed at your interview or a recent appraisal?* **Yes** ☐ **No** ☐

8 *If the company won't finance your training, would you be prepared to finance it yourself?* **Yes** ☐ **No** ☐

9 *Have you attended an in-house training course in the last 12 months?* **Yes** ☐ **No** ☐

10 *Do you receive on-the-job training?* **Yes** ☐ **No** ☐

11 *Are you keeping yourself up to date by reading professional magazines, journals and papers?* **Yes** ☐ **No** ☐

12 *Do you work with others to learn more about their jobs?* **Yes** ☐ **No** ☐

13 *Does your boss coach you on how to improve your performance?* **Yes** ☐ **No** ☐

14 *Are you receiving sufficient training to move on from your current position?* **Yes** ☐ **No** ☐

Summary

- Training keeps the mind alert and open to new ideas, processes and procedures. Training can be in the form of on-the-job training, an in-house or external course, studying for a particular qualification, or learning from peers or supervisors.
- Remember: it is never too late to learn something new. Continuous learning avoids your career stalling because you have stopped your training too early, so don't jeopardize your chances because you haven't the necessary skills.
- Keep yourself up to date and informed, and read about your profession regularly.

7 Business acumen

1 *Do you read the business section of a daily newspaper?* **Yes** ☐ **No** ☐

2 *Do you read the company's literature (in-house publications)?* **Yes** ☐ **No** ☐

3 *Can you name the directors of the organization and their positions?* **Yes** ☐ **No** ☐

4 *Are you aware of the company's financial performance?* **Yes** ☐ **No** ☐

5 *Do you know and understand the company's mission statement?* **Yes** ☐ **No** ☐

6 *Do you avoid openly running down how the business is run?* **Yes** ☐ **No** ☐

7 *Do you see things from another person's standpoint, even though this is sometimes difficult?* **Yes** ☐ **No** ☐

8 *Do you understand how your department interfaces with others?* **Yes** ☐ **No** ☐

9 *Are you a good listener and do you avoid expressing yourself on every subject?* **Yes** ☐ **No** ☐

10 *Are you committed to the company's customers rather than just to serving them?* **Yes** ☐ **No** ☐
If you are committed, you understand the needs and demands of the customers. Often, employees are not even aware of who the customers are.

11 *Are you aware of the company's products?* **Yes** ☐ **No** ☐

12 *Do you know who your company's competitors are and are you aware of their strengths and weaknesses?* **Yes** ☐ **No** ☐

13 *Do you know about the advantages that your company's product or service has over the competition?*

14 *Do you always make sure that you attend the company's briefings?* **Yes** ☐ **No** ☐
Many employees fail to recognize the importance of these and find excuses not to attend them.

Summary

- Companies value employees who have business awareness, who perform their job well and can relate it to the overall function of the business and the environment within which it operates (for example, those who understand how the business performs, how it remains competitive, how it serves the customers, and the company's vision for future growth).
- Do your research and you will become aware of the business as a whole and be able to fit your job into the overall purpose of the company.
- Work with the company, not against it, and in doing so you will make yourself less job specific and more commercially aware.

8 Appraisals

1 *Do you believe appraisals are useful?* Yes ☐ No ☐

2 *Do you prepare in advance for your appraisal?* Yes ☐ No ☐

3 *Do you take a mental or written list of your achievements to your annual appraisal?* Yes ☐ No ☐

4 *Do you take a list of next year's goals to your appraisal?* Yes ☐ No ☐

5 *Are you able to answer the question 'What is your next move?' at an appraisal?* Yes ☐ No ☐

6 *Do you and your manager agree on your next career move?* Yes ☐ No ☐

7 *Do you and your manager agree on the length of time you should spend in your current job?* Yes ☐ No ☐

8 *Do you avoid taking criticisms to heart and work to improve the areas highlighted as weaknesses at appraisals?* Yes ☐ No ☐

9 *Do you feel that the criticisms are fair?* Yes ☐ No ☐

10 *Do you know how to put them right?* Yes ☐ No ☐

11 *Do you feel your appraisals are constructive?* Yes ☐ No ☐

12 *Do you feel your appraisals give you an opportunity to express your opinions?* Yes ☐ No ☐

13 *Do your annual goals get reviewed?* Yes ☐ No ☐

14 *Do you initiate meetings with your boss to review progress made since your appraisal?* Yes ☐ No ☐

15 *Do you feel your boss is being honest in evaluating your potential?* Yes ☐ No ☐

16 *Are you conscious of a recurring theme in consecutive appraisals and do you have a plan to overcome it?* Yes ☐ No ☐

17 *Are you being stereotyped into certain characteristics?* Yes ☐ No ☐

18 *If you are being stereotyped into certain characteristics, are they positive?* Yes ☐ No ☐

19 *Can you be open and honest at an appraisal without any repercussions?* **Yes** ☐ **No** ☐

20 *Does your manager always fulfil promises made at your appraisal?* **Yes** ☐ **No** ☐

Summary

- An appraisal is one of the few times when a manager formally measures his/her subordinate's performance, and the record is then held on file for other managers to view if necessary.
- An appraisal should be a positive meeting, as long as both parties are prepared and behave themselves. Focus on the key issues – your achievements, long-term goals and further on-the-job training – and avoid being drawn into lengthy or negative discussions about relatively unimportant issues. Always agree on the next steps and the timetable for future action.
- If you feel you are performing well within a job, ensure that the manager confirms this and that you are performing in the right areas and direction.
- If you have a grievance against your company and there is no way of resolving it, then it may be time to move on to another organization.

9 The end of the road (vision)

1 *Do you have a target job for the end of your career?* **Yes** ☐ **No** ☐

2 *Do you want your career to take you to retirement? If no, do you have an idea of what you want to do other than enjoy leisure time?* **Yes** ☐ **No** ☐

3 *Do you envisage changing your job before the end of your career?* **Yes** ☐ **No** ☐

4 *Do you want public recognition or to be remembered when you retire?* **Yes** ☐ **No** ☐

5 *Can you imagine the end of the road?* **Yes** ☐ **No** ☐
This will show how far ahead you can plan.

6 *Do you want to be at 'the top' of your profession?* **Yes** ☐ **No** ☐

7 *Do you have an idea of what you want to do after you retire?* **Yes** ☐ **No** ☐

8 *Do you feel you will be satisfied with your career on your retirement?* **Yes** ☐ **No** ☐

9 *Will you have no regrets about your chosen field on retirement?* **Yes** ☐ **No** ☐

10 *When you retire, will you have no personal (family) regrets?* **Yes** ☐ **No** ☐

Summary

- A career vision is a personal plan for the future which is carried out. Avoid having a vision that turns into a fantasy. For example, people often say, 'If I was made redundant I'd set up my own business, change profession or do what I'd always wanted to do' – such a fantasy vision is worthless and also dangerous, because it makes people retreat from the real world into their dream world. They are thus removed from the reality of building their current career and therefore stop being effective in it. To test whether something is a vision or a fantasy, ask yourself why you are not taking action to fulfil it. If you would never pursue this vision, then throw it out and waste no more time thinking about it.

- Remember: if you want something, take action, and if you say something, do it, otherwise time will run out. A career is similar to saving for a pension policy – you can't leave it all to the last minute – so make that change *now*!

10 Current position

1 *Are you seen as an expert in your current position?* **Yes** ☐ **No** ☐

2 *Is your current position a key one with the company?* **Yes** ☐ **No** ☐

3 *Is the position comparable with, graded and rewarded in the same way as those of other people on the same level in your job?* **Yes** ☐ **No** ☐

4 *Do you get invited to meetings to add a valuable contribution?* **Yes** ☐ **No** ☐

5 *Do you ever get invited partway through a meeting to add your view?* **Yes** ☐ **No** ☐

6 *Does this position prepare you for the next step or move?* **Yes** ☐ **No** ☐

7 *Is your current position highly sought after?* **Yes** ☐ **No** ☐

8 *Is there one or a number of successors to your position?* **Yes** ☐ **No** ☐

9 *Is your position secure now and in the near future?* **Yes** ☐ **No** ☐

10 *Is this position an integral part of your career plan?* **Yes** ☐ **No** ☐

Summary

- Remember to perform all of your job – the good, the bad and the really bad. Leave no stone unturned and you will be viewed as a valuable person doing a key job. Excel in your job and it will be easier to move on.

- Experts in their chosen field are invaluable to any business and are rewarded accordingly. Know your subject and read around it, so that you can talk on it with authority. Always express your opinion in a constructive way.

- If your position doesn't equip you with the necessary skills for the next step, then either consider a sideways move to gain broader experience or create opportunities within your current job to gain this experience. Get on courses, volunteer yourself for tasks or put the word around the business.

Improvements to be made

Now write out all the areas that need to be improved under the appropriate heading.

Profession

Career to date

Career planning

Appearance

Money

Training

Business acumen

Appraisals

The end of the road (vision)

Current position

FOUR

The Basic Principles of Career Planning

There are certain basic principles you need to understand and follow in order to be an effective career planner. These will help you to reach your maximum potential and give your career the best chance of success. Before making any changes or planning your future, you need to have an understanding of your career to date, so if you haven't already done so, complete the Career Questionnaire in Chapter 3 without further delay. The answers you give will help you to:

- Look at and assess your career to date.
- See where the gaps lie.
- Pinpoint areas you need to improve or work on.
- Realize what you want to achieve in the long term.

Career planning is similar to planning a journey: you need to know your present location and where your destination is before you can plan your route. An awareness of the 'whole' situation makes it easier to map out the next steps.

Your profession

A career needs a profession. A profession is what you do for a living, what you have spent time training to do or what you want to be doing. It is thus the crux of the career, giving it meaning, purpose and direction. Everyone has a profession, even if they don't perform the job everyday – they may, for example, be doing another job, or be off sick, unemployed, retraining or having a career break – but you can't lose your profession.

THE NEED FOR A PROFESSION

Your profession is part of you. It is what you believe in, associate with, are proud of, are suited to and what offers you long-term growth and satisfaction. In short, it is the mechanism you can use to shine as a person. In order to do things that enrich your life, you need to understand that you cannot separate the work person from the home person, for whatever you do in one area will affect what happens in the other. Because of this, the two areas need to be united and to complement each other – in short, you need to 'live' your profession, as it forms part of you and your future.

Without a profession a career will come unstuck, reach a halt or start to drift off at a tangent. In fact, the career can become a muddle of jobs and bits and pieces that may or may not fit together or have some logic to them. On the whole, however, a career of this sort will have no substance or depth to it, and it will be hard to sell it and convince employers that experience of this sort is beneficial to their organization. With candidates of this kind, employers will tend to read between the lines and see the negative attributes in the person rather than the positive – for example, his/her lack of commitment, related experience, energy, stamina or self-discipline. The person thus invites criticism and makes it easier for employers to reject him/her. Overall, a career without a profession doesn't reflect at all well on the person concerned and will hinder their development.

Children are particularly good at visualizing, referring to and even acting out what they want to be when they 'grow up'. It is a necessary part of their development to live in this timeless world where they can try things out without fear or repercussions, but the key element to their development is the reference to a profession.

As adults, people tend to forget, dismiss or ignore the significance of the profession itself. Having a profession may not be part of their background or educational training; they may start off or get pushed into the wrong profession; or they may not be able to commit themselves to their profession and therefore change company and profession all the time without realizing the implications of their actions. It is a myth to think that if you can do anything and everything you are broadening your chances of career success, because sadly you are not. Employers want someone who can do the job on offer. They want to hire someone who has a clear idea of what he/she wants to do, has a similar background to the vacant job, or has even done this job before somewhere else, so the closer your profession and experience relate to the job on offer the greater your chances of success will be.

The world of work is a serious business, where the stakes are high and everything you do and the decisions you take affect your career and consequently your lifestyle and standard of living. Whereas you might want to take risks associated with your career, however, employers may not want to take the risk with you. They look for employees who have a stable professional background and a willingness to commit themselves to their company, so by recognizing the importance of your profession, and building a career around it you can improve your future opportunities. Anything is possible in the world of work, but just how possible it is for you is dependent upon your self-belief, your drive, your attitude and how well you execute the steps required.

So, brace yourself – for whether you like it or not, you need to have a profession. Then you can turn work from a drudge into something you enjoy!

DEFINING YOUR PROFESSION

You have probably been asked the question 'What do you do for a job?' hundreds of times. What is required is a succinct, clear-cut answer rather than a long-winded, waffly one which means very little at all. Being able to answer this question helps you to visualize, understand and communicate your profession to other people, and if you have an understanding of what your profession is about it will be easier to progress within it.

Firstly, you may say that you are a teacher, nurse, accountant, banker, engineer, tax inspector, buyer, librarian, artist, salesman or whatever. The next stage is to understand the core features of the role itself, for example, the position in the market, the company and its products: to develop within a profession you need to associate with it, hold the same values as your profession and want to learn more about it.

The field

The field or speciality of your work is important in terms of career planning. The field is the way that a person builds up experience within his/her chosen profession. It is important to understand the difference between a profession and a field, because people often confuse the two. For example:

Profession	Examples of fields
Accountancy	Management accounting and reporting
	Financial and corporate accounting
	Ledger and transactional management
	Tax and treasury management

Thus, in simple terms, the field is the speciality of the profession, the bit that makes you *you* and different from the competition.

The field is an indication of a person's experience and is extremely important. Initially in a career it is advisable to build up a broad base of experience, and the way to do this is to change fields regularly. A career, like a tree, needs to have many but strong roots, so it is far more impressive to have a wide experience of the industry/profession you are in than a narrow one. Choose jobs, projects and tasks that force you to increase your knowledge rather than perfect one of your many skills, and try to avoid specializing too early on or you could limit your overall career possibilities. Below a skeleton career path is described which demonstrates these points.

AGE 20–30

Your twenties represent a big decision time. You tend to choose your profession at this time and learn the ropes of that profession. From the jobs you do, you gain an understanding of the organizations you work for and the functions of the business you are in and its competitors. In this decade you not only choose your profession, but often your partner, lifestyle and location of work and home.

AGE 30–40

In your thirties you start to assert yourself within your career. You will build up your key areas of expertise and be exposed to new tasks, which will help you to decide whether or not you want to pursue these in any further depth.

AGE 40–50

In your forties you start to specialize within your career. You develop knowledge, expertise and experience in your chosen fields. You tend to initiate change, and order that change rather than do it yourself. Promotions and job moves happen less often, but when they do they tend to be more substantial and can involve greater personal upheaval and disturbance.

AGE 50+

In your fifties your reputation leads the way. Whether or not you are recognized or valued within your field of work is due to the hard work you have put in during your earlier years. It is the time when people expect to earn high levels of income. The company you work for pays a premium for your reputation, and also for you to shape the business for the future and to develop other employees within the business to carry on after you leave. A harmful attitude in your fifties can lead to derailment, perhaps if you are over-confident and conceited, if you won't work as part of the team, or if you become a liability and tell everyone else how to do and perform their job regardless of whether you understand the role or not!

The outline above follows the typical career path, although not all careers will follow this pattern. It is the fields of work, not the profession, that make up the content and the speciality, so use the fields to become an all-rounder within your profession, and you can then become a specialist. If you have missed out on certain phases, do not panic: you will have to work hard to catch up, but given time and a bit of effort it is possible. And if you want to change profession, you may need to start at the first stage again – good luck!

SPECIALISM

To become a specialist, you need to pursue an area or field of your work in depth. You need to know everything and anything about it, and will then be regarded by your organization as a key source of information.

One of the advantages of specializing within a field is that fewer people do so, so higher salaries can be earned. In addition, the specialist knows the area of work better than anyone else, so he/she can call the shots and dictate more to the company. However, there are also a number of disadvantages. The longer a person sticks in a particular field, the more likely it is that he/she will be typecast in that job forever. This is not a problem if the person's future lies in this role, but often it doesn't. Specialism therefore means that people often unknowingly sacrifice flexibility, because employers fail to see them as capable of doing anything different.

At some stage everyone needs to specialize within their career. However, you should always ensure that you keep up to date, so that you can pre-empt any changes in business practices which could seriously threaten your area of expertise.

Money matters

When planning your career, you can't escape thinking about money. This includes the sort of salary you want to earn and the fringe benefits you require such as company car, petrol paid, private medical insurance, company pension, mortgage benefits, expense account, or anything else that is important to you. The key is to be realistic but to aim high. The figure should reflect your market rate, cover living expenses and leave you room for enjoyment. Remember that employers will assume that if you are at an interview the salary being offered is acceptable to you, but they are usually open to negotiation as long as you can make your case. Talk about figures in terms of your value to the business rather than what you expect to earn.

The company

In planning your career you need to *choose* the kind of company/organization you wish to work for. This narrows down your options and makes it easier to target your applications. It is best to avoid setting your heart on working for certain companies as you are limiting your opportunities, equally, don't reject a company purely on what you have heard but do your own research, as someone else's opinion may not be yours. The following list will help you to make your choice.

- **A large, national or multinational limited or public company**. This is a company where you will be a small cog in a large machine – a company often governed by rules, regulations, the past or someone else (head office or the shareholders), where your influence may be minimal and limited, but this is often offset by better training, promotion prospects and a broader range of job roles. However, career advancement may also mean relocation, perhaps even several times.

- **A smaller, locally headquartered company**. Here you may have a greater say, but less opportunity for advancement and change.
- **A family-owned company or partnership**. This is a company normally run on tradition, hopes and dreams. If your job is in a 'niche' role it is often a good place to work, but family companies can be claustrophobic and if you are not a family member or 'in' with the family it can be restricting.
- **A company known for its social policies**. Here the company's philosophies and attitudes tend to be reflected in the working environment. If you follow these philosophies you will be fine; if not stay away, as you could find it intimidating.
- **A company where your involvement would be minimal**. Here you can clock in at 9 am and leave at 5 pm. Your work life won't encroach on your leisure time.
- **A company where your involvement would be great**. You may even have a chance to become a star. Here it is taken for granted that you will leave only when the job is done, regardless of the time.
- **A company which is highly competitive**. This sort of company will offer you the opportunity for career advancement.
- **A company which is not competitive**. This company offers instead stability and consistency. However, this type of company seems to be encountered infrequently.

Take your pick and then approach those companies that appeal to you. However, it is also worth bearing in mind the following points, as these may influence your career choices.

- Big companies are less interested in a person who has always worked for a small company.
- It is easier to move from a big company to a small company than the other way round.

- There are normally better training facilities within a big company.
- Your influence will be greater in a smaller company.
- Corporate culture will affect your decision. Do you hold the same values as the company, or could you easily adapt?

Changing your profession

The section on profession in the Career Questionnaire in Chapter 3 (pages 39–40) may have convinced you that you want to change your profession. Perhaps you have outgrown it, reached your potential within it or can't commit yourself in the same way as before. However, before you rush to change things it is important to appreciate that there is a difficult road ahead, especially if you have spent many years in another profession.

Changing your profession could be difficult because there will be a lot of learning to do, and it may also be necessary to take a downward step in terms of status, salary and responsibility. The key to changing profession is to find out first whether it is a realistic possibility. Age, sex and/or experience can be barriers to entry into certain professions, so research your desired new profession and establish whether or not it is a possibility for you. Contact the appropriate institutions and careers libraries, or talk to people within the profession itself. Give details of your age, educational background, experience to date and vision for the future; listen to their advice, and only then decide whether or not you still want to make a change that will require a lot of commitment, effort and patience.

BRIDGING THE GAP

The easiest and safest option for bridging the gap between two professions is to change your field of work. Get a foot in the door of the new profession while keeping one foot firmly placed in your existing profession; then, further changes in field can be made once in the new profession in order to build up the necessary experience (see Figure 1 for an example).

The other method which is often used to bridge the gap is to sign on for a full-time study course. This can be an expensive option if you have to pay for your tuition as well as living expenses, so, work out the full costs beforehand. In addition, before committing yourself to this method of retraining you should find out how employers regard this approach; for example, will the technical knowledge compensate for your lack of practical experience in the subject? By tackling this question beforehand you will be able to establish the cost of the course against the payback period. However, if you are off work or having a career break and have the available funds, then this may be a perfect learning option for you (see Figure 2 on page 66 for an example).

Summary

The basic principles of career planning as described in this chapter can be summarized diagrammatically (see Figure 3 on page 67).

Bridging the gap by changing your field of work

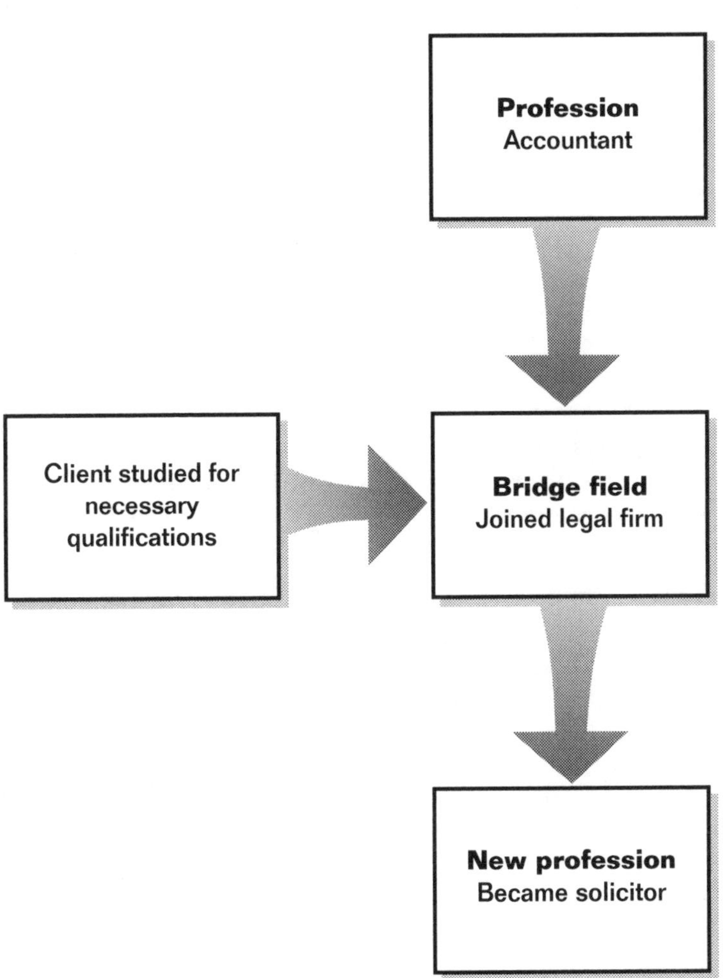

Figure 1

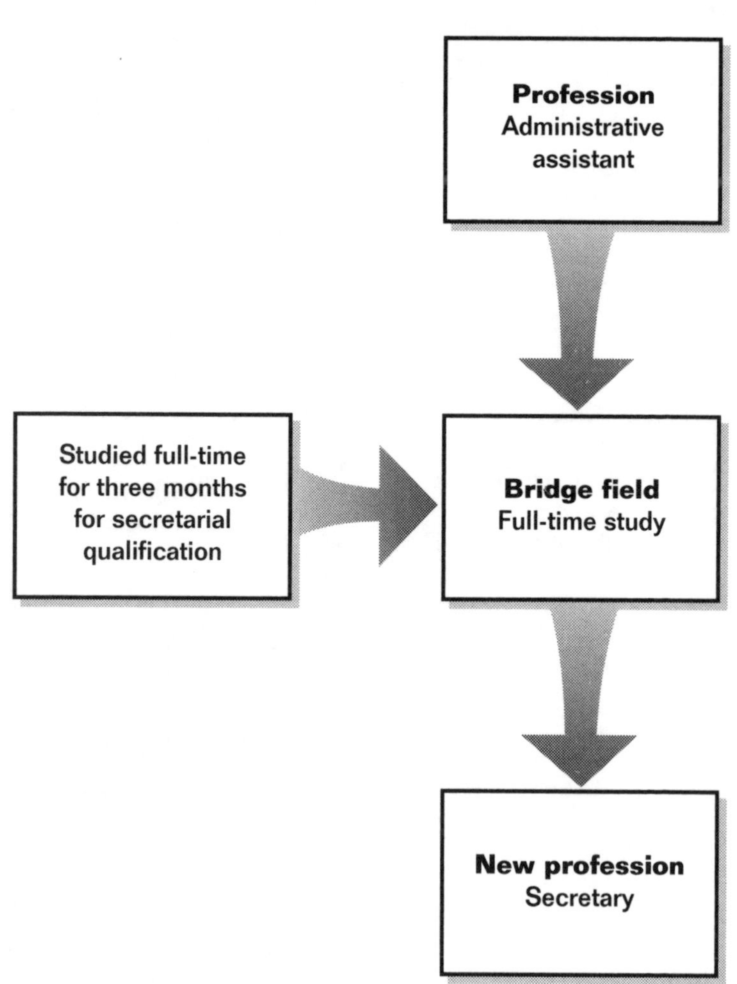
Bridging the gap
through full-time study
Profession
Administrative
assistant
Studied full-time
for three months
for secretarial
qualification
Bridge field
Full-time study
New profession
Secretary

Figure 2

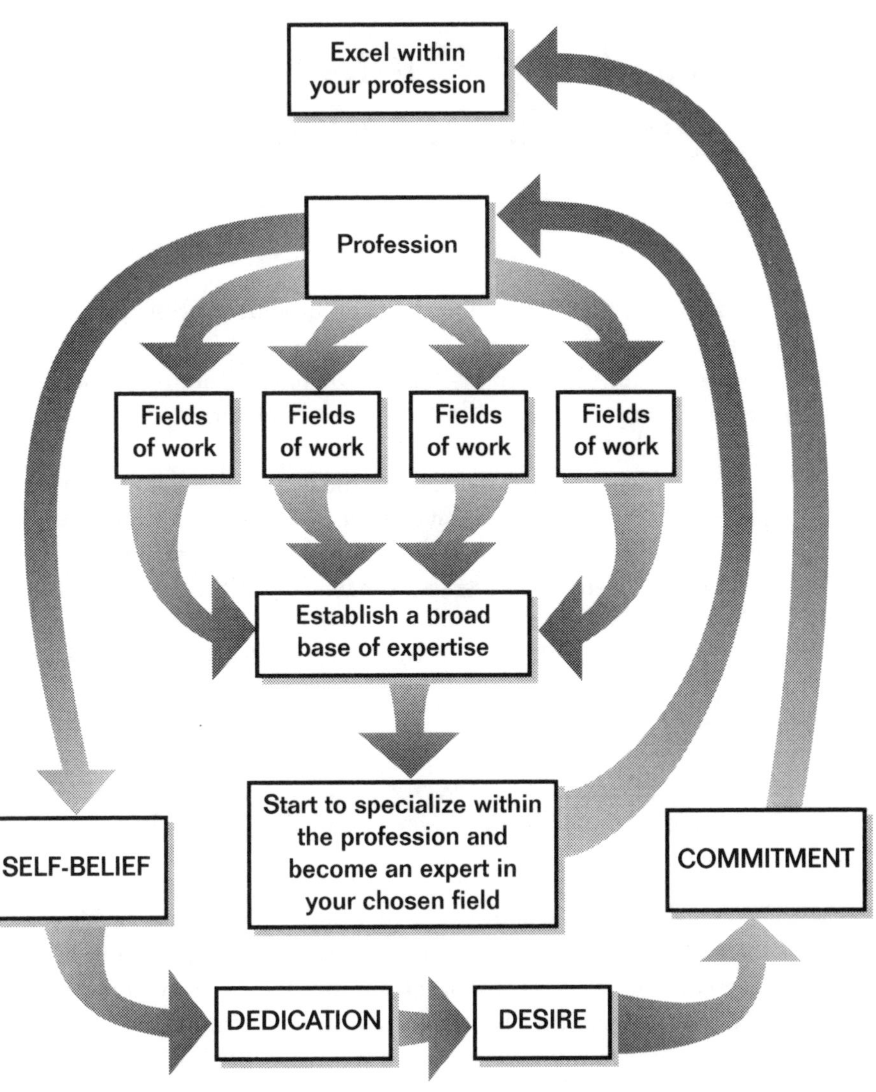
The principles of career planning
Excel within your profession
Profession
Fields of work
Fields of work
Fields of work
Fields of work
Establish a broad base of expertise
Start to specialize within the profession and become an expert in your chosen field
SELF-BELIEF
COMMITMENT
DEDICATION
DESIRE

Figure 3

FIVE

An Easy Route to Your Career Vision

This chapter shows you how to map out your possible career future. This future is reliant upon having a vision of what could be possible for you, as this will push you to take control of your career, encourage personal and technical development and drive you forward.

A vision looks beyond the next job and further down the career path. The reason for this is that a career is vulnerable: anyone can have a few highlights in their job or a few good years, but what will they do when it is all over? So, aim for a career that lasts longer than this and which offers long-term satisfaction and fulfilment. Only you can make the most of your career, so the choice is yours.

Benefits of a career vision

If you develop a vision you will be one step ahead of the competition, because most people think only in terms of their next job move. Usually people want another job in their current company or a job they have seen advertised in national or local newspapers, journals or magazines. The route they take is dependent upon what is available at the time and what appeals in the heat of the moment, and if they can't pull off their job change for whatever reason then despondency, dissatisfaction and disillusionment can set in. This type of vision is one which is here today and gone tomorrow, because people often change their 'vision' totally when they see the latest issue of the newspaper's job page – and they can afford to change their vision all the time because it is not all that important to them, especially if they only thought about it a week ago.

This is a common approach to career planning but without doubt, *you can do better than this*. The good news is that it is not that difficult to develop a vision, as long as you are prepared to adhere to the principles of career planning outlined in Chapter 4 and to do a lot of research. In fact, there may be a substantial amount of research involved if you want to develop the best plan for yourself, but remember that how much research you do is up to you – you are in charge.

Research

The thought of 'research' – the process of finding out all the facts, drawing conclusions and making decisions based upon your findings – may send shivers down your spine. However, the key to successful research is to have an interest in your subject, and this time the subject is you, the market and those people currently performing the jobs you would like, so it is not such a difficult task. The only drawback may be the time you need to invest in pursuing your role as a researcher, so managing your time effectively is important. Listed below are some key points to help you with this.

- View time spent on research as an opportunity to learn and develop your knowledge.
- Avoid 'filling' your time with people, events and tasks that weigh you down. Instead, start to manage and fill your own time, with the aim of furthering your career.
- Accept that you can learn from other people. Show an interest in the people you meet and they will then be more willing to pass on tips and advice to you which will help you to build up your career vision.

- Start using your 'dead' time – lunchtimes and the time before and after meetings or first thing in the morning – to do your research. Use this time to do some reading or meet up with contacts in the profession in order to quiz them on their career and profession to date. Ask general questions such as 'How is your job going?' in order to break the ice, but avoid probing too deeply in terms of pay, perks, bosses and so on, as people can feel threatened by this approach and will not open up to you.
- Be open-minded and don't decide in advance who can or cannot help you, because you don't know until you ask. Keep all your channels of communication open. Write to people in your profession with whom you have lost touch and casually ask them what they are doing now: then arrange to meet up, or talk to them over the phone. Nothing you do is a waste of time, as you never know when what you are doing will come in handy or who will be the most useful person.
- Accept that it will take time to do all the research, but you will need this time in order to think about, imagine and visualize yourself in these jobs.

In order to create a vision you need to practise the technique of visualization based on research, imagining yourself in the role and looking at its functions, responsibilities and profile. Take care to distinguish between the glamour and the actual demands of the job itself.

To work on a vision you need to become absorbed with yourself, your capabilities and your profession. You need to focus on the present moment rather than on the past, because what is past does not have to affect your future. However, most people let their past shape their future because they *choose* to do so, perhaps because their self-worth is damaged or they act out what others predict or say about them.

People form opinions about everyone, which may or may not be based upon accurate information. Mostly, people's opinions are simply *their* perception of a situation. What matters more is whether or not you can rise above other people's opinions and learn to break free by imagining great things for yourself. Glimpse new and different prospects, and above all be creative. The following points will act as useful reminders:

- Be yourself.
- Trust and value your own thoughts, not what other people say.
- Recognize that your feelings count more than what you think you should feel.
- Choose for yourself rather than letting others do it for you.
- Be an individual rather than choosing the safest option.

You must accept that you have enormous personal power to create your future as you wish, but recognize that power is available only in the present.

THE ADVERTISED MARKET

The first research step is to look at the advertised market. This market is enormous, and jobs are advertised in different papers under different sectors. Figure 4 is a reference table showing which profession is advertised in which paper on which day, so use it as a guide. Consider also looking for jobs in the magazines, journals and pamphlets related to your profession.

Your ideal job

You are looking for your 'ideal' job within your profession, the one you want to finish your career doing. Forget about whether you can or can't do it, and just look at this stage. Do you want a high- or low-profile job? Do you want the 'top' job for a managerial role? What sector do you want to work in – private, public or perhaps for a charity? Do you want a development or a functional role? Do you want to be based at home or overseas? The choice is yours!

In fact, you may have an idea of a number of jobs that appeal. This is fine, as long as you have something you can work with and which will act as a signpost for your future. Cut out the advertisements and then file them. When you have had a good look at the market over a period of several weeks, months or even

Figure 4

Where to find newspaper job advertisements

Sector	MONDAY	TUESDAY	WEDNESDAY
Accountancy	Evening Standard Financial Times		Independent
Building/ construction		Daily Express	Evening Standard
Catering/ hotels		Daily Express Evening Standard	
Computing	Independent		Evening Standard Financial Times Times
Creative/ media	Guardian		Evening Standard Times
Education/ courses		Daily Express Daily Mail Daily Mirror Guardian The Herald	Scotsman
Engineering/ technology	Independent		Evening Standard
Finance	Evening Standard		Financial Times Independent
General	Daily Record Evening Standard	Daily Express Daily Telegraph Evening Standard Herald	Daily Record Evening Standard Financial Times
Graduate			
Health	Evening Standard	Independent	
Legal		Times	Independent
Print			
Public Sector	Evening Standard	Daily Express	Guardian
Sales/ marketing	Guardian	Evening Standard Times	Evening Standard Financial Times Independent
Secretarial	Guardian	Daily Express Evening Standard	Evening Standard Times

THURSDAY	FRIDAY	SATURDAY	SUNDAY
Financial Times Times			
Daily Mail			
Evening Standard			
Guardian			
Daily Express Daily Mail			
Independent	Times		
Daily Express Daily Mail Guardian			
Daily Mail Guardian Times			
Daily Express Daily Mirror Daily Star Daily Telegraph Evening Standard Guardian Independent Times	Herald Scotsman	Guardian	Independent Observer Scotland on Sunday Sunday Telegraph Sunday Times Mail on Sunday Sunday Post
Independent			
Daily Mail			
Daily Express Evening Standard Independent Times			
Daily Express Daily Mail Evening Standard	Herald		
Evening Standard Times			

Many of the jobs advertised in these newspapers also appear on the Internet.

a year, you are ready to start to put pen to paper and draw up your version of the ideal job by filling in Figure 5.

The next step is to be clear about *all* the criteria, qualifications and experience required for such a role. Referring to the advertisements for the detail, fill in Figure 6 on page 76 (examples are given in Figure 7 on page 77).

The next stage is to fill in all the 'gaps' between your current job and your desired job , firstly by writing them down and then by setting out to equip yourself with the skills and experience necessary eventually to achieve your ideal job. Remember that if you achieve your ideal job earlier than you expect you will need to develop a vision beyond your original one (this is advisable because it ensures continuous growth). The key criterion in 'filling in the gaps' is to highlight jobs which will *build up your experience in the different fields of the profession*. You will need to look beyond the job title, which can be meaningless as different companies lump all kinds of duties and functions under all kinds of job titles.

Some professions are highly structured and have certain key stepping stones on the route to the top. If you are in one of these professions then it is relatively easy to find out what steps you need to take in order to secure your dream job. For example, the steps for an accountant might be:

- Assistant Management Accountant
- Management Accountant
- Financial Accountant
- Financial Controller
- Divisional Accountant
- Financial Director

If the stepping stones are less clearly defined you will have greater freedom, but you may need to research the market via the people route.

Your ideal job

Current profession

____

Advertisements appeared in

____

____

____

____

____

____

My ideal job is ______________________

In

______________________	Profession
______________________	Job profile

Working for

______________________	Company
______________________	Profile
______________________	Size
______________________	Turnover
______________________	Market
______________________	Salary
______________________	Lifestyle

Figure 5

Qualifications for your ideal job

My ideal job is

____

Qualifications required

Experience required

Background, company and/or sector experience

Personality required

Figure 6

Example of qualifications required for an ideal job

My ideal job is

____

Qualifications required

- Professional
- MBA
- Graduate calibre
- Foreign language

Experience required

- Management
- Development
- Strategic
- 2 years' commercial
- Strong practical skills
- Strong financial skills

Background, company and/or sector experience

- Length of service
- Blue chip background
- Mobility
- European experience
- FMCG organization

Personality required

- Strong communication
- Thorough
- Quick thinker
- Strategist
- Determination to succeed
- Outstanding potential
- Adaptable

Figure 7

THE PEOPLE ROUTE

The people route involves watching, talking to and drawing upon other people's knowledge, reputation and skills. These will be people who are in your profession but who are higher up the career ladder than you are at present, so their position, experience and expertise can help you to further your career. There are several ways in which you can get access to this.

Using people as role models

This aspect is discussed in detail on pages 15–17. When using people in your organization as role models, study how they have acquired the skills and experience that have enabled them to succeed. The most obvious route up through the ranks is not always the best, so remember to think 'wide', or you could end up in a similar situation to that described below and illustrated in Figure 8. In this example, B would be a better choice as a role model than A.

Two people, A and B, were working for the same company. Both were on the same grade in the same profession, but were working in different fields. A, eager for promotion, took the usual career path and got the next job up. B then took A's old job in field 1 to gain broader experience – experience that was vital to the profession as a 'whole'. B was then promoted into field 4, now being on a par with A. When it came to who was to be promoted into field 5, B was chosen because he/she had the broader experience. Even though he/she had initially taken longer to get promoted, he/she had less weaknesses than A for the 'top job'.

Avoid becoming focused on one channel. Remember also that it is easier to change field at the same level than to step down a level, as A would have had to have done if he/she had wanted to acquire such experience, so use your fields to increase your options.

Using people as mentors

A mentor relationship is different to having a role model, because the mentor is not normally your boss but someone higher up than you in the organization who can help you to further your career. The mentor also benefits because he/she is building a reputation

The importance of a broad experience

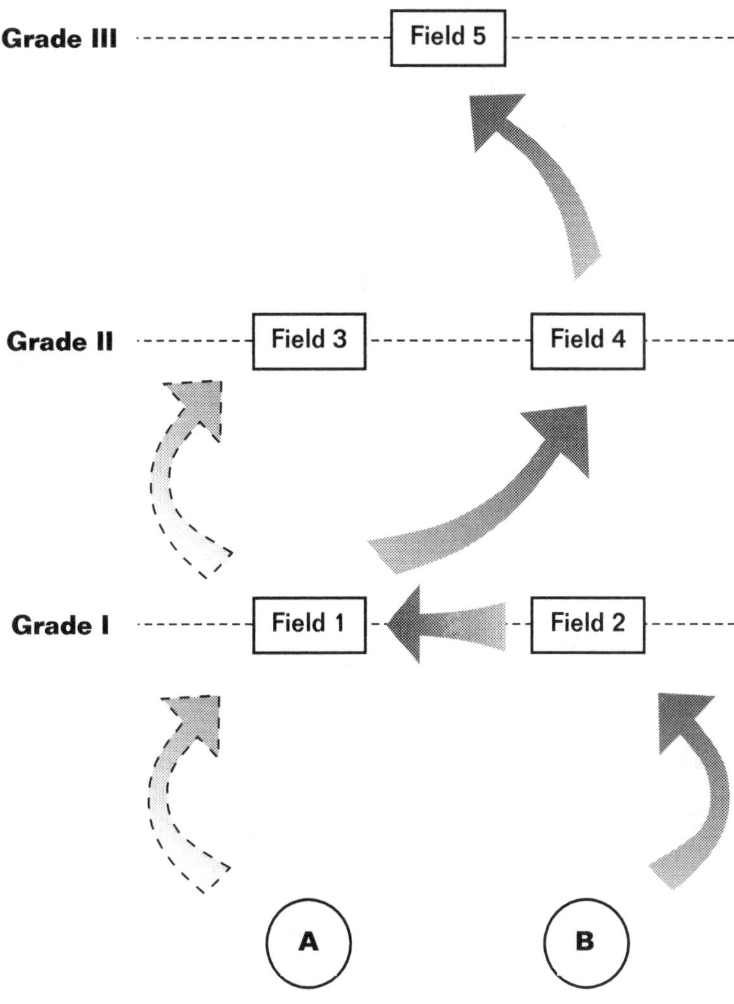

Figure 8

for developing people within the organization. There is no limit to the number of mentors you can have, but avoid having *too* many.

The beauty of having a mentor is that he/she can offer you a confidential and open relationship because the mentor does not appraise the protegé. The protegé can then reveal and discuss in greater depth issues that it may not be advisable to discuss with the role model because they are of a personal, professional, or organizational nature, or even about the boss him/herself. The role of the mentor is to advise, encourage and talk from personal experience, but you should never rely too heavily on him/her. With a mentor you can discuss issues such as:

- Career development and progression.
- Working relationships with colleagues and senior management.
- The culture and politics of the organization.

Cultivate and develop a personal, confidential and beneficial relationship with your mentor. Use him/her as a source of knowledge and do not be afraid to discuss your vision and the possible steps to achieve it with your mentor. Mentor relationships will eventually come to an end, but that is normally because both parties choose to move on or to end the relationship. Try to lessen the blow of your mentor leaving by developing another relationship before this one ends.

Shadowing key people

Shadowing is a subtle form of research. As the word implies, your presence is subtle but hardly visible. Shadowing people means that you watch, observe and assess other people's behaviour, attitudes and actions. As part of your training, you may have had the opportunity to 'shadow' people and watch them performing certain duties before you were let loose on the job; within a job, you can now create these types of opportunities for yourself. Either use contacts you already have, or ring up or write to people within your profession who you think could be of assistance to you. Explain that you would like to know more about their job, its duties, functions and responsibilities, as a role of this sort is a possible next career step for you. Try to visit this person in their place of work in order to see them at work and to have a detailed chat about careers. Most people will be flattered that you have shown an interest in them and therefore will be willing to help you and talk about their job.

You can also shadow in your place of work. You can do this in meetings, in a group environment, at professional committee meetings or when you are on site visits. Note how these key people conduct themselves. What qualities do these people have that you lack? How do other people respond to them? Are they respected or feared? How have they gained their experience, knowledge and reputation? What is their background? Would you like to be in this person's job? Can you gain the qualities you require in order to perform this job? What is this person's vision for the future?

In the work environment people can feel threatened if others probe too deeply, so be careful. Observe the person for a while and then ask your questions. If they won't answer them, is it a matter of not knowing the answer or of not wanting to tell you? If the person puts up barriers and won't give you answers to certain questions, do not be put off. Find someone else and ask the same question and they will almost certainly respond differently and probably provide you with the answer.

Shadowing is a vital way of obtaining information. Try to find out as much as you can about the particular role you are interested in. There is nothing like first-hand experience of a job; shadowing could provide you with the insight you need, and at an interview you will be able to talk about experience rather than your perception of the job. In short, shadowing will provide you with the opportunity to look before you leap, so give it a go – it could be a worthwhile investment.

Networking

Start to network in order to further your career. Networking is the process of meeting, talking to, and mixing with people within your profession. The purpose of it is to promote yourself, find out about the people you meet and other companies, and to keep up to date with the job market. There is no certainty about when a business or suitable career opportunity will arise, but networking will increase your knowledge and reputation within the right circles, so make the most of it.

Meeting new people can be both daunting and exciting, and how you cope with new situations, relate to new people and interact with them depends upon your self-image and experience of mixing with people. Some people are instinctively good at promoting themselves in areas where they will be noticed and open to new career initiatives, while others have consciously to develop this skill. However, it is vital to be able to communicate with people in order to further your professional career, so listed below are the key points to remember.

- **Be aware of and respond to the environment**. Try to mingle and speak to people rather than standing around on your own. It is no longer considered rude or pushy to introduce yourself to others, so avoid being shy, because if you do choose to wait for other people to make the first move you could be waiting for a long time! If people don't respond to you or, even worse, reject you, then that is their problem not yours; try not to take it personally, and find other people to talk to. However, avoid interrupting intense one-to-one conversations as this will not be appreciated. Instead, find a bigger group to join and try to fit in with the group as a whole. When circulating, try to leave a group politely, for example by saying that you must go and talk to a particular person. Remember that it is rare for business people to be rude, because they are in the business of making contacts as well, so it is worth taking a few risks – you may be more successful than you thought possible.

  On your departure from the occasion, always thank the host genuinely or follow up with a thank-you letter afterwards. If you are the host, try to meet and greet the guests warmly. It also helps if you can introduce people with mutual areas of interest, referring to their names, the companies they represent or something for which they are known.

- **Be genuinely interested in other people**. Hold eye contact with other people and look interested in what they are saying, rather than looking over their shoulder in order to find someone else you could go and talk to. Remember to listen to what the person is saying rather than just waiting for them to finish talking so that you can start again. Build upon what is being discussed and make sensible, valid and appropriate contributions. After all, good networking is about remembering the person the next time you meet and being able to refer to what he/she told you last time.

A good way of remembering people is to write something down on the back of their business card or in the file where you store all your cards. Then, the next time you ring this person you can refer to the discussions of your previous meetings, and cultivating business relationships of this sort can turn transitory conversations into long-lasting and trustworthy relationships. Try to be as interested in other people as you are in yourself – it is not easy, but if you can do it people will warm to you.

- **Try to be part of the group**. Give everyone an opportunity to talk rather than hogging the stage. People tend to view attention seekers of this kind in a negative light.
- **Talk about yourself**. You want people to remember you, too, so introduce yourself by stating your name, your profession, and the company you work for. Refer when possible and appropriate to your areas of expertise, so that your audience can build up a truthful and healthy picture about you, and one that you have communicated rather than one that is made up on the basis of the audience's perceptions.
- **Be alert**. You have to be in the mood for networking in order for it to be effective, so go to functions, events and gatherings in the right frame of mind as you never know when an opportunity will fall into your lap. If you are alert, you will be able to grasp that opportunity.

Where can you network?

The answer to this question is that you can network anywhere. The most effective form of networking is to have a combination of planned and unplanned meetings; the key is to achieve the right balance for you. Read the list below and see if you can increase your networking possibilities.

- Join professional clubs, institutions or work-related associations.
- Follow up contacts you have in the profession. Ring or write to them in order to get back on terms again.
- Network with people you work with during lunch hours or after work.
- Go to functions you have been invited to.
- Get yourself on the mailing lists of professional magazines so that you can find out what is going on and where.
- Call in on your contacts if you are in the vicinity or driving past. Make people feel that they are important to you and they will then reciprocate. Share information and help each other.
- Be accessible and available for friends and colleagues. Try to agree mutually convenient arrangements.
- Contact your college or university and update them on your career to date. Attend and support their functions and activities, and make and establish new relationships at these events. Draw upon the university's source of information about companies and the key people in those organizations whom you may need to meet in order to support your career.

The networking list is almost endless. Good networkers will know people involved in key operations and will be able to create opportunities for themselves when required. They will use their contacts to their advantage, and their reputation in the profession will open the necessary doors. In short, value the power of networking.

You should use whichever method is needed – the advertised market route, or the people route, or both – in order to create, live and implement your vision. The key is to trust your own instincts and to be committed to your vision. Developing a career vision can take a long time, so above all be patient. Wishing won't make anything happen, so at some stage you will have to take the first step forward, and each step will lead you towards your overall vision. So – is it possible for you?

SIX

Self-assessment

This chapter is designed to assess and measure how strong an applicant you are for the job on offer. It contains a simple exercise for you to complete, which gives you the opportunity to take a long, hard look at yourself – the whole 'self'. From the results, you will learn which aspects of yourself you are satisfied with and which may need to be worked on, as these negative aspects may be letting you down at present.

Listed overleaf are the factors which differentiate you from the competition. Award yourself the following scores as appropriate.

Give yourself 3 points for every factor you class as **excellent**, 2 points for every one you think is **above average** and 1 point for every one where you think you are **on a par with other applicants**. Award no points for your **liabilities.**

Personal details

SCORE

Consider things such as your age, sex, location and family circumstances.

Personality

SCORE

Do you have the appropriate personal skills for the job on offer? Are you in the right frame of mind, because attitude is important?

Work experience

SCORE

Is your company background and work experience in line with what is required?

Qualifications

SCORE

Do you have the appropriate qualifications for the job on offer?

Your CV

SCORE

Is your CV targeted towards the job? Does it demonstrate your key capabilities, strengths and achievements?

Interview skills

SCORE

How competent are you at being interviewed? Do you enjoy it, hate it or get really nervous? Above all, is the 'real' you coming across at the interview?

Personal skills

SCORE

These are skills applicable to your application such as language skills, PC skills, driving ability, business skills and knowledge of your work environment.

Communication skills

SCORE

The ability to write and to communicate a message verbally.

SCORING: LIABILITY 0, ON A PAR 1, ABOVE AVERAGE 2, EXCELLENT 3

Presentation skills SCORE

The ability to stand in front of an audience, large or small, and communicate your message.

Social skills SCORE

The ability to meet, mix and network with others in a professional and courteous way.

Appearance SCORE

The ability to present and promote yourself in the business environment and to ensure that you are well-groomed.

Voice quality SCORE

The ability to vary your pace, pitch and tone and project your voice.

Handshake SCORE

The ability to reflect a warm, friendly and confident greeting through your handshake.

Eye contact SCORE

The ability to look at and show an interest in people but to avoid staring at them.

Posture SCORE

The ability to adopt a comfortable, positive and confident stance, standing upright, keeping your shoulders relaxed and your feet still rather than shifting from side to side.

Fitness SCORE

Are you in good shape and still able to pace yourself through the day? Do you have a healthy physique and a visible smile?

SCORING: LIABILITY 0, ON A PAR 1, ABOVE AVERAGE 2, EXCELLENT 3

- **If you scored fewer than 10 points**, you are giving the competition an easy ride. You are throwing away many opportunities.
- **If you scored 11–16 points**, you are an average applicant, offending few but impressing few as well.
- **If you scored 17–32 points**, you are an above average applicant but still have some weakness in key areas.
- **If you scored 33–48 points**, you are an excellent applicant who has developed the whole self. You have the advantage of appreciating the need to be an all-round performer and to be strong in every area. You may have learned these techniques from others or from courses, by reading or by being observant of your colleagues. Keep up the good work.

Whatever your score, you are now aware of any weaknesses you may have, and awareness is the first step towards improvement. You deserve the best for yourself and your career, so anything you have marked as being a liability or on a par with your competitors is not good enough. You will need to sort these things out – and there is no time like the present. Remember, though, that the career strategist makes adjustments not just to fit in but to succeed, so develop your skills throughout your career.

SEVEN

Drivers and Restrainers

Sometimes a job simply doesn't hold the same attraction when it is actually yours! This point has been hinted at in Chapters 4 and 5 in terms of seeing a job for what it really is, visualizing yourself actually performing the tasks, and living with the vision for a while to see whether the job has the same 'pull' for you. The reason for this is to avoid damaging your credibility by making the wrong career choices. The key is to take time to decide upon your job changes and to see the move for what it is, rather than what you want it to be.

The way to do this is to view the move as a whole rather than looking at isolated bits and pieces. Some people make the mistake of bundling together all the good bits about the new job and comparing these with all the bad bits of their current job. This is shortsighted and will inevitably lead to oversights or nasty shocks and surprises. You need to appraise the new job fairly; to do this, you need to be aware of what it is that is motivating you to change your job, and also to measure what you will gain from your new job against what you are giving up in your current one.

It is also beneficial to be aware of what your career 'restrainers' are. These are the things which are holding you back or preventing you from excelling in your career, and they could continue to restrain you unless you implement some improvements or changes. You may be prepared to take the action required, but if not then at least you are aware of the weakness and in the end you will probably reach a level of acceptance of the reason behind your refusal to change – for example, a person's desire to stay in the same area may be more important to them than the upheaval, uncertainty and stress involved in moving house for a new job.

The idea of the exercises which follow is to make you aware of *your* drivers (motivations) and restrainers. To carry out the exercises, rank the listed words and phrases in order of importance to you on a scale of 1 to 10. If you can't choose between two words or phrases, keep them together. In some of the exercises there is also a short-term/long-term choice. Mark item one with a tick, indicating whether it is a short-term or long-term gain or problem. The chart on page 95 shows you how to fill in all your findings on one page so that you can take an overview of the whole situation.

Drivers for change

Establish what is driving you to change your job by ranking the following words and phrases on a scale of 1 to 10. Number 1 represents your most important motivator for change and number 10 your least important among the selected words. If necessary, replace words with ones which are more closely applicable to your situation.

- Pay/status of job
- Responsibility of job
- Internal/external recognition
- Relationship with boss
- Profession/job content
- Possibility of progression
- Relationship with colleagues/team
- Personal achievement
- Supervision/leadership style and effectiveness
- Physical conditions and location of work

1 ______________________________

2 ______________________________

3 ______________________________

4 ______________________________

5 ______________________________

6 ______________________________

7 ______________________________

8 ______________________________

9 ______________________________

10 ______________________________

New job gains

To assess the effectiveness of a possible job move, rank the following job gains on a scale of 1 to 10 as well. In addition, decide whether each gain is long or short term. Again, change any words necessary in order to make this exercise a personal one.

- Company profile, reputation, site or structure
- Technical/professional or practical experience
- Job profile whether internal, external or both
- Promotion or enhanced package
- Responsibility of role
- Freedom to change, implement or influence procedural practices
- Culture/creativity and philosophies of the business
- Product prestige/ image or market position
- A future in terms of careerdevelopment,progression and advancement
- Opportunity to do what is important to you (perhaps to be different, build up a new skill or try something new)

New job gains		Long-term	Short-term
1	______________	☐	☐
2	______________	☐	☐
3	______________	☐	☐
4	______________	☐	☐
5	______________	☐	☐
6	______________	☐	☐
7	______________	☐	☐
8	______________	☐	☐
9	______________	☐	☐
10	______________	☐	☐

Job losses

What do you give up by changing your job? Listed below are ten of the most typical job losses. Do any of these apply to you, and if so, are you prepared to give them up? As for job gains, rank these losses on a scale of 1 to 10 and decide whether they are long or short term.

Reputation, influence and authority within your current department or company.

Job security. Remember that the devil you know is often better than the devil you don't!

Knowledge of the business, the company and the procedures of the organization.

Comfort and stability. You can probably cope with the demands and stress of your current role.

The people you work with, your boss, your subordinates and even your competition.

The particular working environment, for example your office and your working relationships.

Your personal attachment to the current job, whatever it may be.

Company benefits, perhaps in the form of pay, car, canteen, flexi-time, expense account, private medical insurance, company pension, staff social activities and facilities.

Convenience of company location, journey time to and from work, mode of transport, and facilities such as car parking.

The company's 'name', prestige or position within the market.

	Job losses	**Long-term**	**Short-term**
1	______________________	☐	☐
2	______________________	☐	☐
3	______________________	☐	☐
4	______________________	☐	☐
5	______________________	☐	☐
6	______________________	☐	☐
7	______________________	☐	☐
8	______________________	☐	☐
9	______________________	☐	☐
10	______________________	☐	☐

Restrainers to change

Listed below are typical career restrainers. Read the list of words and phrases and pick out which, if any, apply to you. Rank them in order of importance from 1 to 5 and note whether or not each is a permanent or semi-permanent restrainer.

- Personality/attitude
- Experience/technical expertise
- Area/mobility
- Family/partner
- Presentation:CV/interview skills
- Desire to learn
- Procrastination/never get round to it
- Money and pressures on home finance
- Need for security
- Self-esteem/self-belief

		Permanent	Semi-permanent
1	______________________	☐	☐
2	______________________	☐	☐
3	______________________	☐	☐
4	______________________	☐	☐
5	______________________	☐	☐

Transfer your conclusions from all four sections on to the chart opposite to help you view all aspects of your situation and job move.

You can use this detailed and practical approach to make career choices based upon all the available facts rather than upon emotions, perceptions or hearsay. Practise and master this technique and making that ultimate job choice will be a lot easier.

Drivers for change

1	____________	6	____________
2	____________	7	____________
3	____________	8	____________
4	____________	9	____________
5	____________	10	____________

New job gains

		Long-term	Short-term
1	____________________	☐	☐
2	____________________	☐	☐
3	____________________	☐	☐
4	____________________	☐	☐
5	____________________	☐	☐
6	____________________	☐	☐
7	____________________	☐	☐
8	____________________	☐	☐
9	____________________	☐	☐
10	____________________	☐	☐

New job losses

		Long-term	Short-term
1	____________________	☐	☐
2	____________________	☐	☐
3	____________________	☐	☐
4	____________________	☐	☐
5	____________________	☐	☐
6	____________________	☐	☐

7	______________________	☐	☐
8	______________________	☐	☐
9	______________________	☐	☐
10	______________________	☐	☐

	Restrainers to change	Permanent	Semi-permanent
1	______________________	☐	☐
2	______________________	☐	☐
3	______________________	☐	☐
4	______________________	☐	☐
5	______________________	☐	☐

EIGHT

The Next Move

Your next career move may now be firmly on the agenda. As any move involves careful planning, thought and consideration, don't rush at it. Give yourself time to explore, assess and decide upon the best option for you. The possibilities are listed below.

- Explore your current role. Assess your current performance to date, the future of the role and whether or not you could increase the responsibilities or profile of the role itself in order to increase your long-term options.
- Consider a job with the same company but in a different field.
- Explore the advertised job market.
- Explore the unadvertised job market.
- Equip yourself with the right job-hunting tools. Write a CV which sells your key skills and expertise, and practice your interview technique – *sell* yourself into your next job.

Once you have decided on which direction to take, stick to it. Keep lots of irons in the fire and be persistent. Remember that most people don't have a firm idea of what job they are looking for and consequently they don't achieve it, so resist the temptation to be like everyone else. Get a firm idea of what job you want and set about achieving it. Active job hunting is what is required, and the key is to keep at it even if it appears to be taking a long time. Securing a new career move can take anything from one month to a few years: a contact of mine took six years to secure the 'right job', and he invested those six years in building up the experience he required for that job. He got the job of his dreams in the end because he was shrewd enough to acquire the necessary skills and patient enough to wait that long! The key is to be cunning, rational and logical in your decision-making – in short, be different from the competition, because that in itself will get you noticed.

Your current job

The most important thing to remember is that it is better to make a job change only when you have nothing left to offer your current job or role. For example, you may have 'outgrown' it; you may need extra stimulation; responsibility, prestige or reward; or you may have achieved or exceeded what was required – in short, you have performed the role to your highest potential.

Many people do not meet this crucial criterion before they start to think about or even to make job changes, because they simply don't realize the importance of it. They are after a short-term gain in salary or position, or can't face up to what they are running away from (which might be extra responsibility, certain people in the organization, having to put in extra effort, learning a new skill or doing something they don't want to do). However, unless you have performed within a role you will be only 'half-cooked'; half-proficient, half-capable, half-knowledgeable, half-experienced or half-respected, and ultimately only half-rewarded by your new organization. You must therefore avoid making a career change too early, because if you move before the time is right then your gain may only be slight and you could have put more effort into building your reputation somewhere else.

ASSESS YOUR PERFORMANCE

How do you feel about your current job and your performance? An advertisement for your job tomorrow in a national newspaper would highlight all the good points about it, other people would want it and before long the position would be filled. You need to assess whether this job still holds the same attraction for you and whether it is really in your best interests to stay put.

Are you good at what you do? It is important to look at your job as a whole, not just the nice bits, for you will never be a success if you can only do bits of a job well. What you are after is a complete picture so that you can spot any weaknesses in your experience which may need to be put right before your next move.

What do you do in your current job? You will need to draw up a list of your key duties as below, referring if necessary to your job description, and then mark each duty with a tick in one of the columns to indicate how well you carry out the task. The following questions will help you to make up your mind:

- Do you feel confident performing the task?
- Do you take a longer or a shorter time than others to do the task?
- Would extra training help you?
- Could you teach someone else how to do the job?

	Duties include	Never carried out the duty	Performance	
			Average	Above average
1	______________	☐	☐	☐
2	______________	☐	☐	☐
3	______________	☐	☐	☐
4	______________	☐	☐	☐
5	______________	☐	☐	☐
6	______________	☐	☐	☐
7	______________	☐	☐	☐
8	______________	☐	☐	☐
9	______________	☐	☐	☐
10	______________	☐	☐	☐

(Add or remove lines as necessary.)

In order to be a star performer and worthy of promotion, you need to be scoring above average for most, if not all, of your essential duties. Write down what needs to be improved and against each one indicate a realistic timescale.

	Improvements	Timescale
1	______________________	________
2	______________________	________
3	______________________	________
4	______________________	________
5	______________________	________

(Add or remove lines as necessary.)

The next step is to focus on what you have achieved within the job. Achievements increase your value to a company and distinguish you from the competition and prospective employers will primarily be interested in this area.

Now is the time to take stock of how well you are performing within the job. Concentrate on what you have contributed to your role. To help jog your memory, focus on what you have been commended for and what positive feedback you have had from your boss and others within the organization. Include as many achievements as you can and indicate with a tick in one of the columns whether the achievement made a slight or a considerable improvement.

	Achievements include	Slight improvement	Considerable improvement
1	______________________	☐	☐
2	______________________	☐	☐
3	______________________	☐	☐
4	______________________	☐	☐
5	______________________	☐	☐

(Add further lines as necessary.)

The key is to remember that it will be very difficult to convince a prospective employer to offer you the job unless you have achieved and reached your full potential within your current role, so if you haven't already done so, start achieving now. Be committed to improvement and try to avoid putting off doing certain tasks. Are you procrastinating over:

- Difficult and unpleasant tasks?
- Tasks that don't fit easily into your daily routine?
- New and challenging tasks?

Everyone procrastinates from time to time or puts obstacles in their own way, but the best way to stop procrastinating is to do it *now*. Commit yourself to the task, start it and then finish it. It takes time to improve, so avoid being too hard on yourself – celebrate your successes and keep working towards your overall plan. You will get there in the end, so for now focus on performing within your current job.

DOES YOUR JOB HAVE A FUTURE?

Despite everything that has been said above, it is sometimes necessary for people to move jobs when they are only 'half-cooked', especially if their job future is vulnerable (employers tend to be more lenient towards the individual under these circumstances). Establish whether your job has a future by answering these.

- Is your job likely to be axed in the future?
- Is yours a vital role in the running of the organization?
- Does the establishment need you or are you easily replaced?
- Are you an expert in your field?
- Does your future within this role excite you?

If your future is vulnerable, make the change before you are forced to look for work.

Expanding your role

Under some circumstances, a change of job may not be possible. For example, you and your partner may both have a career, so geographical options may be limited; organizations are now slimmer, so opportunities are fewer; or your company may not operate a job rotation system. However, don't panic, because the other option is to develop your current role and enhance your expertise and value. Listed below are some possible options:

- **Focus on the importance of your role**. Take pride in your work and start to feel that your role is important. If something is important to you, you will not want to fail at it, and in turn not wanting to fail at something draws out your potential. Realize also that hardship or failure can be an important time for reflection and for assessing your resilience and perhaps your personal faults.
- **Take ownership of what you do**. Being responsible and accountable will help you to focus on the importance of what has to be done. It will also force you to think about how things can be changed or improved rather than relying on others to do this.
- **Work with new or more people, or both**. Work with a variety of people on different projects and try to learn from them. They may be role models for you or be able to show you how certain characteristics, behaviour or values operate within the business environment.
- **See pressure as an opportunity rather than a threat**. Resist the temptation to panic and try to let pressure such as tight deadlines, heavy workloads or longer hours bring out the best in you.
- **Increase the variety of your work**. Variety can be working at a different pace, dealing with large amounts of information, coping with change or working with lots of people. Dealing with unfamiliar situations can help you to be more relaxed under these circumstances and to juggle lots of things at any one time.

- **Recognize that other people's opinions do count**. Whether you like it or not, you are being watched and assessed, so, try to develop your 'political' skills by adapting your opinions and behaviour accordingly.
- **Develop your resourcefulness**. This is the ability to give something a go and to ensure that your project succeeds. Try enlisting support by influencing people into your way of thinking or negotiating favourable terms.
- **Think strategically**. Learn to think in terms of the whole organization rather than just your job.
- **Pinpoint the missing element**. This is the ability to recognize what is missing in a project, process or assignment. Management support, key skills, technical knowledge or equipment can all be the missing pieces in the jigsaw.

You can use these strategies to develop your role further.

Changing fields

When making a job change, always ensure that you have considered the option of changing your job by changing your field within the same company (see pages 66–7). The advantage of changing fields is that you can broaden your experience, hold on to your reputation but also increase your value within the same company. Is changing fields a suitable option for you?

The advertised/unadvertised job markets

If you have excelled within your current job and there are no openings within your company, then you will have to look externally for a job. Refer to the list of newspaper advertisements on page 72–73 to increase your options.

JOB APPLICATIONS

Whether via a CV or an application form, a job application needs to focus on making you look a winner. Listed below are the key points to remember when applying for jobs using the employer's application form.

- **Read through the form first and think about it**. Don't just dash it off.
- **Draft your answers**. Don't be tempted to copy your last application form blindly, merely updating the information slightly. Each application should be tailored to the job on offer.
- **Focus on making yourself look a winner**. Never assume that your worth is known. Concentrate on writing about how your skills will add value to the employer, and mention any relevant courses or outside activities. Employers are looking for certain qualities including enthusiasm, commitment and a display of personal initiative. Even if you find it hard to demonstrate these qualities in your professional life, mention how you use them in your personal life; for example, you may have completed a distance learning course or been on an 'outward bound' course. Work and home life go hand in hand and your skills are your life skills, so mention them.
- **Answer all the questions**. It is vital not to leave any gaps or to write 'see attached CV' on your application form. This is simply not good enough. You may have already completed hundreds of applications, but you are after the job, and it is up to you to fill in the form properly.
- **Fill in the form neatly**. To avoid errors and smudges, take a photocopy of the form, and fill this in first, making sure that your answers are not squashed up. Leave the completed

form for a day or two and then re-read it. Have you done yourself justice? Is what you have said relevant and legible? Can you read it easily, and is there enough space between the lines for the employer to write his/her comments?

- **Note the closing date**. Closing dates are not there for fun, so make sure you send off your form in time or you may not be considered for the job at all!

YOUR CV

A good CV will create opportunities for you in both the advertised and unadvertised job markets. An employer is not employing a qualification, he/she is employing you – the whole person. If you can come across as positive, enthusiastic and with much to offer, you are more likely to create interest. Look at your existing CV. If it has a poor layout, is difficult to follow or is full of spelling mistakes, then start again. Listed below are the key points to note in compiling a good CV.

- **Be brief**. Avoid writing more than is truly necessary.
- **Keep your CV to two pages**. A CV is more likely to be read and remembered if it is short and relevant.
- **Avoid the personal pronoun ('I')**. The CV has your name at the top so it is obviously about you. Instead, use the third person verb (e.g. 'organized' rather than 'I organized'). This is far more powerful than using 'I' or 'one'.
- **Include only relevant information**. Your CV will be more effective if it is targeted towards the job. No employer wants to read through pages and pages on you, so mention only what is truly relevant. You can always expand on details at an interview.
- **List all your achievements**. You want to convey the impression of someone who succeeds and contributes to different environments, so list them all.

- **Refrain from mentioning salary or references until your interview**. Keep all your options open at this stage and wait until you are in a position to negotiate favourable terms.
- **Avoid being negative in your CV**. Don't dwell on why you left a job or on any negative issue as it won't enhance your chances.

Realize that you may need a different CV for each of your job targets. A good CV is worth whatever time and effort it takes, so it is worth getting it right. Remember also that if you lose a potential job through a weak CV you are doing yourself a grave disservice. (For further details on compiling a CV, see *How to Write a Perfect CV in a Weekend,* also in this series.)

UNADVERTISED JOBS

The unadvertised job market is enormous and can represent as much as 75 per cent of the total job market. The unadvertised job market is literally what it says: jobs which are available but never publicly advertised. More and more people are now turning to this type of job hunting as the usual advertised route is becoming so competitive. The way to win through the unadvertised route is to create a list of personal contacts and to personalize speculative applications.

Personal contacts

Initially, you need to create your own list of personal contacts. These will be people you know who can do any of the following:

- Offer you a job.
- Advise you of a job opening.
- Tell you about someone who could offer you a job.

Everyone has these kinds of contacts, but not everybody uses them. In most cases, pride or embarrassment prevent people from approaching others. People often want to feel that they can get a job through their own efforts rather than by relying on someone else, but you will need to disregard this and concentrate on securing the best job possible.

Creating a list of contacts

Consider anybody who might be able to help you as a contact. Initially, ask the people closest to you – your family, relatives and friends – for the names of people who could help in your job search. Try to be specific in your requests, for example: 'I am looking for a . . . position, within a . . . sized company'. This approach avoids the embarrassment of people thinking that you are really after money or a loan and indicates clearly how they can be of assistance to you, even if all they can do is keep their ears and eyes open.

The next level of contacts is people with whom you have already had some personal contact. These could be business contacts past and present, former bosses, your old college/university tutors and fellow students, your banker, lawyer, doctor, dentist, people you mix socially with, or anyone who you have or have had dealings with. Write a list of all the people and next to each name write down how they can help you. Write to or phone them, asking perhaps for a name of someone who might be able to help you. Avoid being put off if the answer is 'No'. Keep trying, and remember that even if you have called 30 people it may be the thirty-first who can help, so keep at it.

When you send your CV to a contact or write a speculative application, always include a personalized covering letter. Introduce yourself, and where applicable say who has given you this person's name, for example: 'I have been referred to you by (person's name), who mentioned your company is looking for . . . .' If you are writing a speculative letter, always talk about the company first, for example: 'I read your article in . . . magazine and I was interested to read that you do . . .'. Then, highlight your key areas of experience and expertise, and end the letter by telling the person that you will ring them or call in to see them.

In summary, you need to ensure that your next career move is your *best* move, so enlist the support of your boss, your current company or your contacts to ensure that you achieve it!

NINE

Conclusion

The onus is on you to make your career fulfil your dreams and expectations. Focus your energy on your attitude, building relationships with your boss and colleagues, and learning from people around you. Give yourself time to think things through, to develop your vision for the future and to become a real expert at your job. Remember that it is you, not others, who is in charge of your destiny. Whatever you want – go and get it. It is up to you!

Planning is vital to your career success. However, before making any career move you should always:

- **Check that this is the right step for you.** Take your time to think about the new job, for a hasty, ill thought-out career move is likely to be a bad one. A poor reputation could haunt you for a long time, so talk to colleagues, tutors and mentors, and listen to their advice. The key is to select and not just accept your jobs – but always trust your instincts.

- **Ensure that the job offers you the opportunity to build up new skills.** Just like a tree, you need to have solid roots and this will stand you in good stead for the future. Don't be tempted to specialize too early on, as it could be difficult to change direction at a later date. There is no prescribed route that you have to follow, so don't get too hung up on what you think you ought to do. What is more important is to build up a portfolio of valuable skills and achievements and create a reputation of which you can be proud.

Planning your career will reduce some of the job-searching stresses, but each situation will have its unique set of challenges – challenges which you are now ready to meet!

Index